IMPACT!

Adult Reading and Language Skills

Book 2

Janice C. Motta
Reading Specialist
Dean of Continuing Education
Bristol Community College

Kathryn L. Riley
ESL Specialist
Coordinator of ESL Program
Roxbury Community College

▲▼ ADDISON-WESLEY PUBLISHING COMPANY
Reading, Massachusetts • Menlo Park, California
Don Mills, Ontario • Wokingham, England • Amsterdam
Sydney • Singapore • Tokyo • Madrid • Bogota
Santiago • San Juan

for Evelyn M. Carbone
Arnold A. Carbone
Edward P. Riley

ISBN: 0-201-05313-6
GHIJ-AL-89

TO THE TEACHER

Impact! is a three-level ESL reading skills development program designed to be used in conjunction with any ESL series. *Impact!* is also a powerful teaching tool to use with native speakers who need to master reading skills. The program uses a sight-word approach tested and proven most effective with adult beginning readers. *Impact!* is unique in that it guarantees success to students by controlling grade level, grammatical structures, and required reading skills, while presenting adult topics and survival vocabulary to ensure motivation. Numerous illustrations provide helpful context clues for understanding vocabulary. Writing, speaking, and listening skills are integrated into the program as well.

Book 2 of *Impact!* is intended for students who are beginning adult readers. It is written at Grade Levels three and four, according to the Fry Readability Scale. Book 2 of *Impact!* was designed for use as a sequel to Book 1 of *Impact!* However, it can also be used independently of that book, provided that the student is reading at Grade Level three and has accomplished a low-intermediate level in ESL instruction. Use the placement test in the Teacher's Guide for Book 1 of *Impact!* to determine whether the students are ready for Book 2 of *Impact!*

Book 2 of *Impact!* is divided into four units, each of which presents in context different sets of choices that are both relevant and challenging to adults. Reading objectives and ESL structures that are realistic to adult beginning readers are given prior to each Unit in the student text. These goals provide the students with an overview and reference point as to what they can achieve as they proceed through each Unit of Book 2 of *Impact!* Review this crucial information with the students to make sure that they have oral knowledge of the grammatical structures.

The successful use of Book 2 of *Impact!* is predicated on the fact that the students are comfortable using the vocabulary and grammar in each lesson. Do not begin any lesson until the vocabulary and grammar have been mastered orally. The Appendix in *Impact!* Book 2 has an alphabetical list of the vocabulary from *Impact!* Book 1 for the students to review.

Use of the Teacher's Guide for Book 2 of *Impact!* is recommended. It provides step-by-step directions, as well as follow-up and enrichment activities, for effective use of the student text. In addition, the Teacher's Guide features answer keys and discussion ideas.

CONTENTS

UNIT ONE
Everyday Choices

Lesson 1

Where to Eat

Lesson 2

Where to Shop

Lesson 3

**How to Save at the
Supermarket**

Lesson 4

Which to Buy

Student Reading Objectives

1. to recognize and read the following letter combinations: *ch, cl, ea, fr, gh, oo, ou, sh, sp, st, wh*
2. to understand the denotative meaning of everyday advertisements
3. to recall specific information
4. to write and understand the meaning of relevant vocabulary

ESL Information

The following intermediate-level grammatical structures are used and practiced for the first time in Unit One.

1. *like* + a gerund (I like going to the zoo.)
2. past modal: *could* (I could swim last year.)
3. past modal: *had to* (I had to go to the doctor yesterday.)

A review of the simple present and present continuous tenses also appears in this Unit.

It is 12:30 P.M. You are in Middletown. You want to eat there. You want pizza. Where can you eat?

OR

It is 5:00 P.M. You are hungry. You want to take out food and eat it in your house. Where can you buy this food?

OR

It is Sunday. You want to eat dinner in a restaurant. You want to drink wine with your food. Where can you eat?

Exercise 1: Careful Reading

Directions: Look at the page from the phone book. Write the names of the right restaurants.

1. Which restaurants serve pizza?

    a. *Pizza Palace*   b. _____

2. Which restaurants serve lunch?

    a. _____   b. _____

    c. _____

3. Which restaurants serve dinner?

    a. _____   b. _____

    c. _____   d. _____

    e. _____   f. _____

4. Which restaurants are open on Sunday?

    a. _____   b. _____

    c. _____   d. _____

5. Which restaurant serves Chinese food?

    _____

6. Which restaurants serve seafood?

    a. _____   b. _____

7. Which restaurants serve complete Italian dinners?

    a. _____   b. _____

8. Which restaurants serve food to take out?

    a. _____   b. _____

    c. _____

Exercise 2: Deciding

Directions: Look at the page from the phone book. Check (✓) the right answer.

	Open at 5:00 P.M. yes	Open at 5:00 P.M. no	Take Out yes	Take Out no
1. Seaside Wharf	✓	____	____	✓
2. Jade Dragon	____	____	____	____
3. The Snapping Claw	____	____	____	____
4. The Pizza Pan	____	____	____	____
5. Pizza Palace	____	____	____	____
6. Italian Villa	____	____	____	____

It is 5:00 P.M. You are hungry. You want to take out food and eat it in your house. Where will you buy this food? _____

	Middletown yes	Middletown no	Lunch yes	Lunch no	Pizza yes	Pizza no
1. Seaside Wharf	____	____	____	____	____	____
2. Jade Dragon	____	____	____	____	____	____
3. The Snapping Claw	____	____	____	____	____	____
4. The Pizza Pan	____	____	____	____	____	____
5. Pizza Palace	____	____	____	____	____	____
6. Italian Villa	____	____	____	____	____	____

It is 12:30 P.M. You are in Middletown. You want to eat there. You want pizza. Where will you eat? _____

	Open Sunday		Serves Dinner		Serves Wine	
	yes	no	yes	no	yes	no
1. Seaside Wharf	___	___	___	___	___	___
2. Jade Dragon	___	___	___	___	___	___
3. The Snapping Claw	___	___	___	___	___	___
4. The Pizza Pan	___	___	___	___	___	___
5. Pizza Palace	___	___	___	___	___	___
6. Italian Villa	___	___	___	___	___	___

It is Sunday. You want to eat dinner in a restaurant. You want to drink wine with your food. Where will you eat? _____

Exercise 3: Understanding Sounds

A. Directions: Read these.

e + a = *ea* as in h<u>ea</u>t   w + h = *wh* as in <u>wh</u>ere

c + h = *ch* as in <u>ch</u>eck   or w + h = *wh* as in <u>wh</u>o

B. Directions: Circle the word with the same sound as the letters underlined.

1. pl<u>ea</u>se	are	seafood
2. <u>ch</u>icken	cash	Chinese
3. <u>wh</u>at	why	wrote
4. m<u>ea</u>t	eating	wear
5. <u>ch</u>ange	children	clerk
6. <u>wh</u>ich	when	wrote
7. <u>wh</u>o	writing	whose

11

Exercise 4: Understanding Words

Directions: Study the pictures and the words. Write the words.

1. beer and wine *beer and wine*

2. pizza _____

3. seafood _____

4. Chinese food _____

5. Italian food _____

Exercise 5: Understanding Sentences

Directions: Read the sentences. Look at the pictures. Match them. Write the right number next to each picture. Then copy the sentence.

1. Ja Lee is eating pizza.
2. Tom is drinking wine.
3. This restaurant is open daily.
4. Sarah is eating Chinese food.
5. Malik is eating seafood.

Example:

4   *Sarah is eating Chinese food.*

Exercise 6: THINK

Directions: This exercise is about you. Check the right answer.

	Yes	No	I don't know
1. I like going to restaurants.	_____	_____	_____
2. I like eating pizza.	_____	_____	_____
3. My father is eating Chinese food now.	_____	_____	_____
4. My mother is cooking at home now.	_____	_____	_____
5. I like eating in restaurants on Sundays.	_____	_____	_____
6. My brother likes drinking wine and beer.	_____	_____	_____
7. My father likes eating at home.	_____	_____	_____
8. I like eating hamburgers for lunch.	_____	_____	_____
9. My sister likes eating eggs for breakfast.	_____	_____	_____
10. I like shopping in a supermarket.	_____	_____	_____
11. I am studying in school now.	_____	_____	_____
12. I am talking on the telephone now.	_____	_____	_____
13. I like eating in expensive restaurants.	_____	_____	_____
14. I like eating in cheap restaurants.	_____	_____	_____

Lesson 2 **Where to Shop**

Exercise 1: Careful Reading

Directions: Look at the signs. Write the right answer.

Example:

1. How much are the apples?   Where do they cost less?

   The Market Place ____*98¢*____   *Goody's Grocery*_____

   Goody's Grocery ____*89¢*____

2. How much are the eggs?   Where do they cost less?

   The Market Place ____ ____   _____

   Goody's Grocery _____

3. How much is the tomato soup?   Where does it cost less?

   The Market Place _____   _____

   Goody's Grocery _____

4. How much is the fish?   Where does it cost less?

   The Market Place _____   _____

   Goody's Grocery _____

Exercise 2: Deciding

Directions: Look at the shopping lists. Answer the questions.

A.

1. How much will it cost at The Market Place?

apples	_____
eggs	_____
fish	_____
TOTAL	_____

2. How much will it cost at Goody's Grocery?

apples	_____
eggs	_____
fish	_____
TOTAL	_____

3. Where will you buy your food? _____

B.

Shopping List
3 cans of tomato soup
3 lbs. apples
1 doz. eggs

1. How much will it cost at The Market Place?

tomato soup _____

apples _____

eggs _____

TOTAL _____

2. How much will it cost at Goody's Grocery?

tomato soup _____

apples _____

eggs _____

TOTAL _____

3. Where will you buy your food? __ _____

Exercise 3: Understanding Sounds

A. Directions: Read these.

s + h = *sh* as in <u>sh</u>oe   g + h = *gh* as in ei<u>gh</u>t

s + p = *sp* as in <u>sp</u>end

B. Directions: Circle the word with the same sound as the letters underlined.

1. <u>sp</u>eak   special   soup

2. daug<u>h</u>ter   eight   enough

3. ni<u>gh</u>t   morning   neighbor

4. <u>sh</u>irt   skirt   she

5. <u>sh</u>op   stop   shoe

6. <u>sp</u>in   spill   sell

19

Exercise 4: Understanding Words

Directions: Study the pictures and the words. Write the words.

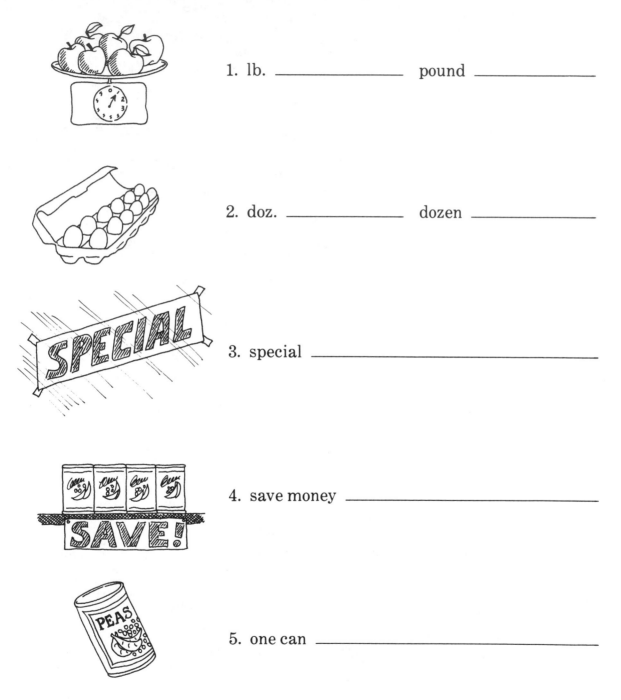

1. lb. _____ pound _____

2. doz. _____ dozen _____

3. special _____

4. save money _____

5. one can _____

Exercise 5: Understanding Sentences

Directions: Read the sentences. Look at the pictures. Match them. Write the right number next to each picture. Then copy the sentence.

1. Please give me a pound of apples.
2. Lena is buying a dozen oranges.
3. I need four cans of tomato soup.
4. Goody's Grocery is having a special sale.
5. Save on chicken this week.

_____ _____

_____

_____ _____

_____

_____ _____

_____ _____

_____ _____

Exercise 6: THINK

Directions: This exercise is about you. Check the right answer.

	Yes	No	I don't know
1. I eat apples	_____	_____	_____
2. I buy fish.	_____	_____	_____
3. I eat pizza for lunch.	_____	_____	_____
4. I drink wine with dinner.	_____	_____	_____
5. I study at night.	_____	_____	_____
6. I read at night.	_____	_____	_____
7. My friends talk a lot.	_____	_____	_____
8. My mother buys food on sale.	_____	_____	_____
9. My father buys clothing on sale.	_____	_____	_____
10. My grandmother cooks with tomato soup.	_____	_____	_____
11. I like eating in restaurants.	_____	_____	_____
12. I like my family.	_____	_____	_____
13. I go shopping on Friday.	_____	_____	_____

STORE COUPON   40¢

Save 40¢ on

your next purchase of

**HEAVEN'S BLEND
COFFEE**

TO CONSUMER. This coupon good only on the product
indicated. Only one coupon redeemed per purchase. Any
other use may constitute fraud. Coupon not transferable.

40¢   HEAVENLY FOODS COMPANY

OR

60¢ ──── STORE COUPON ────

SAVE 60¢

on any size jar of
ENJOY! coffee

Limit — One coupon per purchase

──── TASTY PRODUCTS, INC. ────   60¢

STORE COUPON

SAVE 30¢

WHEAT
POWER CEREAL

30¢

on your next purchase of

WHEAT
POWER CEREAL

Dandy Foods, Inc.

STORE COUPON

SAVE 35¢

when you buy

SUDSY
Detergent

SUDSY
Detergent

ONE 10 lb., 11 oz. or
ONE 5 lb., 4 oz. or
ONE 49 oz. (3 lb., 1 oz.) or
THREE 20 oz. (1 lb., 4 oz.)

35¢   *Fine Goods Corp.*

STORE COUPON

Save 20¢

on

SOFT + SOAPY SHAMPOO

SOFT + SOAPY SHAMPOO

20¢   *Fine Goods Corp.*

STORE COUPON

Save 12¢

when you buy **2** Bath Size bars
or **2** Super Size bars or
3 Regular Size bars

SCRUB-A-DUB

SCRUB-A-DUB

SCRUB - A - DUB
Soap

Limit one coupon per purchase

TASTY PRODUCTS, INC.

12¢
OFF 2

STORE COUPON

40¢

Save 40¢ on

your next purchase of

HEAVEN'S BLEND
COFFEE

HEAVEN'S BLEND COFFEE

HEAVEN'S BLEND COFFEE

TO CONSUMER. This coupon good only on the product
indicated. Only one coupon redeemed per purchase. Any
other use may constitute fraud. Coupon not transferable.

40¢   HEAVENLY FOODS COMPANY

24

Exercise 1: Careful Reading

A. Directions: Look at the coupons. Write the right number.

1. Which coupon is for soap? _____

2. Which coupon is for detergent? _____

3. Which coupon is for shampoo? _____

4. Which coupon is for coffee? _____

5. Which coupon is for cereal? _____

B. Directions: Look at the coupons. Answer these questions.

1. How much are you going to save on the soap? _____

2. How much are you going to save on the
   detergent? _____

3. How much are you going to save on the
   shampoo? _____

4. How much are you going to save on the coffee? _____

5. How much are you going to save on the cereal? _____

Exercise 2: Deciding

A. Directions: Look at the coupons. Check the right answer.

	RICE		WHEAT		BRAN		OATS	
	yes	no	yes	no	yes	no	yes	no
Coupon 1	___	___	___	___	___	___	___	___
Coupon 2	___	___	___	___	___	___	___	___
Coupon 3	___	___	___	___	___	___	___	___

B. Directions: Read the paragraph. Look at the coupons. Write the answers.

    Yesterday, Lil wanted to buy cereal for her family. Her
son does not like rice cereal, and her daughter doesn't
like wheat cereal. Her husband doesn't like bran cereal.

1. Which cereal could Lil buy? _____

2. By using a coupon for the cereal, Lil saved _____ .

26

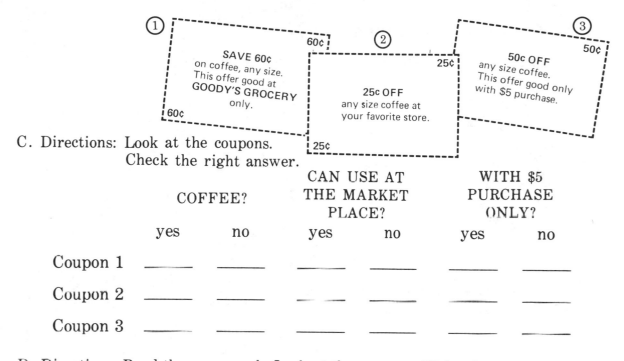

C. Directions: Look at the coupons.
Check the right answer.

	COFFEE?		CAN USE AT THE MARKET PLACE?		WITH $5 PURCHASE ONLY?	
	yes	no	yes	no	yes	no
Coupon 1	___	___	___	___	___	___
Coupon 2	___	___	___	___	___	___
Coupon 3	___	___	___	___	___	___

D. Directions: Read the paragraph. Look at the coupons. Write the answers.

Ben shopped at The Market Place yesterday. He bought a pound of coffee. It cost $2.85. He did not want to buy anything else. He wanted to use one of the coupons.

1. Which coupon could Ben use? _____ _____

2. By using the coupon for the coffee, Ben saved _____ .

Exercise 3: Understanding Sounds

A. Directions: Read these.

o + u = *ou* as in y<u>ou</u>   o + o = *oo* as in afterno<u>o</u>n

o + u = *ou* as in bl<u>ou</u>se

B. Directions: Circle the word with the same sound as the letters underlined.

1.	afterno<u>o</u>n	bedroom	now
2.	bl<u>ou</u>se	counter	coupon
3.	y<u>ou</u>	soup	house
4.	<u>ou</u>r	too	out

Exercise 4: Understanding Words

Directions: Study the pictures and the words. Write the words.

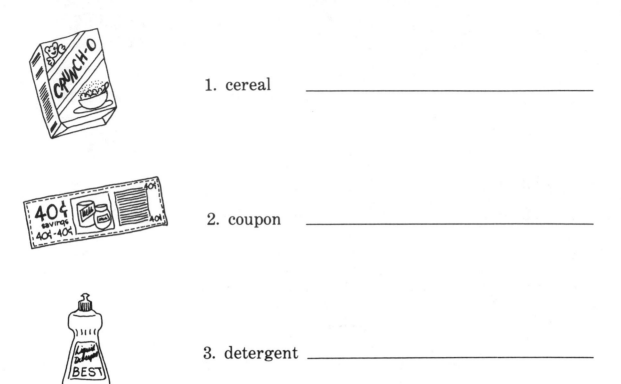

1. cereal _____

2. coupon _____

3. detergent _____

4. shampoo _____

5. soap _____

Exercise 5: Understanding Sentences

Directions: Read the sentences. Look at the pictures. Match them. Write the right number next to each picture. Then copy the sentence.

1. Makiko's son is eating his cereal.
2. The detergent is next to the sink.
3. Arturo cut the coupon out of the newspaper.
4. Marlene washed her hands with the soap.
5. This new shampoo makes my hair look good.

_____ _____

_____

_____ _____

_____

_____ _____

_____

_____ _____

_____

Exercise 6: THINK

Directions: This exercise is about you. Circle the right answer.

1. I can speak English well.   yes   no

2. I could speak English well last year.   yes   no

3. I can read and write in English.   yes   no

4. I could read and write in English last year.   yes   no

5. My mother or my father has to cook breakfast
   every morning.   yes   no

6. I had to cook dinner last night.   yes   no

7. I have to get up early every morning.   yes   no

8. I had to get up early Sunday morning.   yes   no

9. I could drive a car last year.   yes   no

10. I had to go to work this morning.   yes   no

11. I could pay all my bills last month.   yes   no

12. I had to pay all my bills last month.   yes   no

Lesson 4 Which to Buy

OR

SAVE $20.99

$99 our reg. $119.99
SAVE $20.00

Atlas Brand

Black & white TV.
12 in. picture.
Quick start picture tube.

$79 our reg. $99.99

Gold Brand 12 in. AC/DC portable
black & white TV

Compact, lightweight, perfect for
viewing at home or away.
Earphones and screen.

You want to buy a television set. You
look for newspaper ads every day. Today
you saw two ads. Which TV is a better
buy?

BIG D

BUY NOW!

Magnet Brand
black and white TV
16 in. picture.

$179

SAVE $20.99

$79 our reg. $99.99

Gold Brand 12 in. AC/DC portable
black & white TV

Compact, lightweight, perfect for
viewing at home or away.
Earphones and screen.

SAVE MART

our reg. $119.99
$99 SAVE $20.00

Atlas Brand

Black & white TV.
12 in. picture.
Quick start picture tube.

TODAY'S BEST BUY

SOSHA BRAND black and white TV
Big 21 in. picture. You can bring it
home for only $229!

32

Exercise 1: Careful Reading

A. Directions: Look at the BIG D Advertisements for television sets. Answer these questions.

1. What is the size of the Gold Brand TV picture?   _____

2. What is the regular price of the Gold Brand TV?   _____

3. What is the sale price of the Gold Brand TV?   _____

4. How much can you save on the Gold Brand TV?   _____

B. Directions: Look at the SAVE MART advertisements for television sets. Answer these questions.

1. What is the size of the Atlas TV picture?   _____

2. What is the regular price of the Atlas TV?   _____

3. What is the sale price of the Atlas TV?   _____

4. How much can you save on the Atlas TV?   _____

5. Which store—BIG D or SAVE MART—is selling cheaper 12-inch televisions?   _____

C. Directions: Look at the BIG D and SAVE MART advertisements. Circle the right answer.

1. The Magnet Brand TV screen is bigger than the Gold Brand TV screen.   yes   no

2. The Atlas Brand TV screen is the biggest.   yes   no

3. The Sosha Brand TV screen is smaller than the Atlas Brand TV screen.   yes   no

4. The Gold Brand TV screen is the smallest.   yes   no

5. The Magnet Brand TV is cheaper than the Gold Brand TV.   yes   no

6. The Gold Brand TV is cheaper than the Atlas Brand TV.   yes   no

7. The Atlas Brand TV is the cheapest.   yes   no

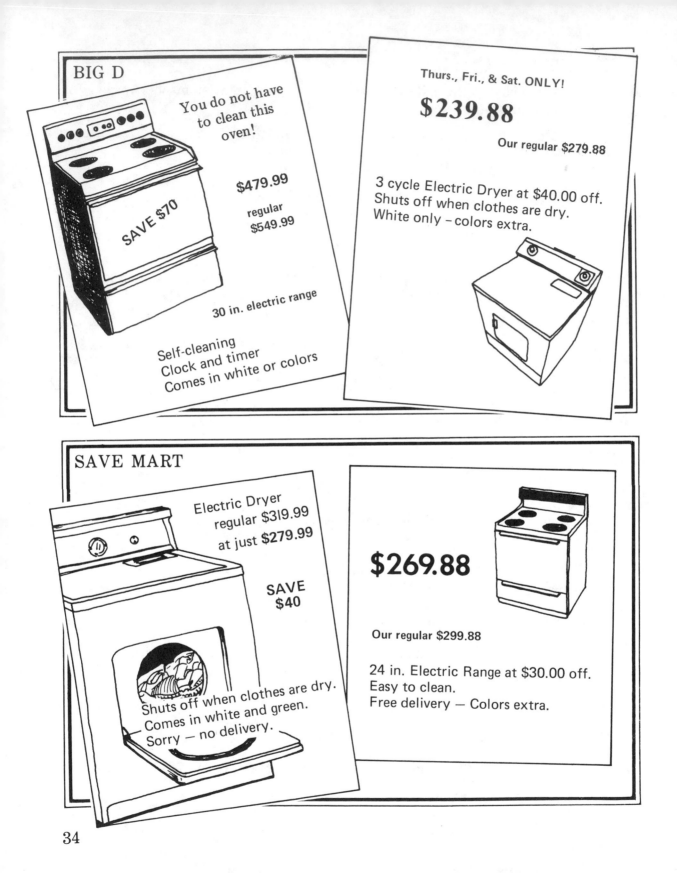

BIG D

You do not have to clean this oven!

$479.99

regular $549.99

SAVE $70

30 in. electric range

Self-cleaning
Clock and timer
Comes in white or colors

Thurs., Fri., & Sat. ONLY!

$239.88

Our regular $279.88

3 cycle Electric Dryer at $40.00 off.
Shuts off when clothes are dry.
White only – colors extra.

SAVE MART

Electric Dryer
regular $319.99
at just $279.99

SAVE $40

Shuts off when clothes are dry.
Comes in white and green.
Sorry — no delivery.

$269.88

Our regular $299.88

24 in. Electric Range at $30.00 off.
Easy to clean.
Free delivery — Colors extra.

Exercise 2: Deciding

> Mr. and Mrs. Smith are going to buy a new electric range. They want to buy a green one because they have a green refrigerator. There are four children in the Smith family. The Smiths need a large oven to bake for the family. No one in the Smith family likes to clean ovens. Which stove are Mr. and Mrs. Smith going to buy?

A. Directions: Look at the electric range ads from both stores. Check the right answer.

	Big D yes	Big D no	Save Mart yes	Save Mart no
1. Does anyone have to clean the oven?	____	____	____	____
2. Are colors an extra charge?	____	____	____	____
3. Does it have a large oven?	____	____	____	____

4. Which stove are the Smiths going to buy? _____

Exercise 3: Understanding Sounds

A. Directions: Read these.

$f + r = fr$ as in <u>fr</u>iend $c + l = cl$ as in <u>cl</u>asses

$s + t = st$ as in <u>st</u>op

B. Directions: Circle the word with the same sound as the letters underlined.

1. <u>fr</u>om   for   front
2. <u>st</u>udy   store   suit
3. <u>fr</u>iend   floor   free
4. <u>cl</u>erk   clean   cheap
5. <u>st</u>ation   set   start
6. <u>cl</u>othes   call   clothing

Exercise 4: Understanding Words

Directions: Study the pictures and the words. Write the words.

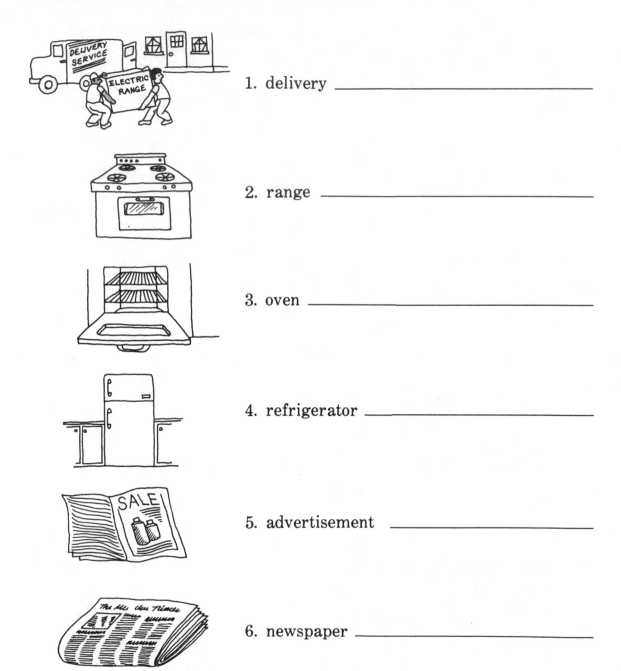

1. delivery _____

2. range _____

3. oven _____

4. refrigerator _____

5. advertisement _____

6. newspaper _____

Exercise 5: Understanding Sentences

Directions: Read the sentences. Look at the pictures. Match them. Write
the right number next to each picture. Then copy the sentence.

1. Assad is going to use the new stove.
2. The young girl can read the newspaper.
3. The advertisement is for coffee.
4. The meat and fish are in the refrigerator.
5. That woman is making a delivery.

Exercise 6: THINK

Directions: This exercise is about you. Check the right answer.

	Yes	No	I don't know
1. My mother has an electric range.	——	——	——
2. My father likes cooking on his electric range.	——	——	——
3. I had to cook on an electric range last night.	——	——	——
4. I like shopping at sales.	——	——	——
5. I don't like cleaning electric ranges.	——	——	——
6. I like saving money.	——	——	——
7. My mother likes baking.	——	——	——
8. I like baking.	——	——	——
9. My father likes baking.	——	——	——
10. I like watching television.	——	——	——
11. I bought a television last year.	——	——	——
12. I could understand the English on the television last week.	——	——	——

Exercise 1: Careful Reading

Directions: Look at the ads from the phone book. Write the answers.

1. Which restaurant serves Chinese food?

   a. _____

2. Which restaurants serve food to take out?

   a. _____   b. _____

3. Which restaurants serve lunch?

   a. _____   b. _____

   c. _____

4. Which restaurant serves dinner nightly from 5:00?

   a. _____

Exercise 2: Understanding Sounds

Directions: Circle the word with the same sound as the letters underlined.

1. pl<u>ea</u>se   are   seafood
2. <u>ch</u>ange   clerk   children
3. dau<u>gh</u>ter   enough   neighbor
4. aftern<u>oo</u>n   bedroom   now

Exercise 3: Understanding Words

Directions: Match the pictures and the words. Write the right word next to each picture.

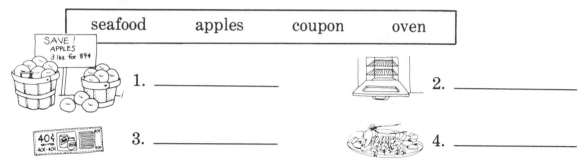

seafood   apples   coupon   oven

1. _____   2. _____

3. _____   4. _____

Exercise 4: Understanding Sentences

Directions: Write each sentence next to the right picture.

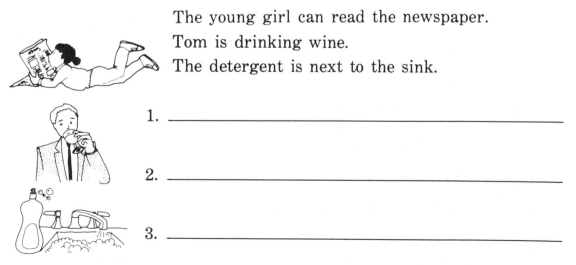

The young girl can read the newspaper.
Tom is drinking wine.
The detergent is next to the sink.

1. _____

2. _____

3. _____

UNIT TWO
Important Choices

Lesson 5

Where to Work
At Home or Away from Home

HOUSE FOR SALE

10-year-old house 6 rooms,
3 bedrooms, new kitchen,
with fireplace,

FOR RENT

5-room apartment for rent,
3 bedrooms, new carpet in
living room, $250 per month
includes heat and hot water.
Call after 5:00 p.m.
241-8314

Lesson 6

How to Live
To Buy or Rent Housing

Lesson 7

What to Drive
To Buy a New or Used Car

Student Reading Objectives

1. to recognize and read the following letter combinations: *gr, br, ai, th, pr, tr, tw, dr*
2. to understand the denotative meaning of newspaper advertisements
3. to recall specific information
4. to write and understand the meaning of relevant vocabulary

ESL Information

The following intermediate-level grammatical structures are used and practiced for the first time in Unit Two.

1. reflexive pronouns: *myself, yourself, herself, himself, themselves*
2. present perfect tense
3. present perfect tense contrasted with simple past tense
4. infinitive structure with: *want, decide*

CASHIERS WANTED

Part-time and full-time jobs.
Make your own schedule.
Starting salary $4.25 per hour.
Apply at The Market Place.

an equal opportunity employer

OR

Marie does not want to work away from home. She wants to stay home and be a full-time homemaker.

Exercise 1: Understanding Words

Directions: Read the definitions. Write the words.

1. less than
   full-time   part-time   _____

2. 8 hours a day
   5 days a week   full-time   _____

3. pay for
   work   salary   _____

4. a person who
   works at home   homemaker   _____

5. work done
   at home   housework   _____

6. not working
   for pay   unemployed   _____

7. a plan for
   your time   schedule   _____

Exercise 2: Understanding Sentences

Directions: Read these sentences. Read the definitions again. Then write
the right word.

1. Jane works in the morning from 9:00 A.M. to 12:00 noon.

   She works _____ .

2. Ilya works all day from 7:00 A.M. to 3:00 P.M. He works

   _____ .

3. John's _____ is $3.50 an hour.

4. Lily works at home. She is a _____ .

5. Sam does not have a job. He is _____ .

6. Wanda cleans the kitchen and washes the clothes. She does

   _____ .

7. I planned my time last week. I made a _____ .

Exercise 3: Careful Reading

CASHIERS WANTED

Part-time and full-time jobs.
Make your own schedule.
Starting salary $4.25 per hour.
Apply at The Market Place.

an equal opportunity employer

Marie does not want to work away from home. She wants to stay home and be a full-time homemaker.

Directions: Read the page. Read each sentence carefully. Look at the example. Then check the right answer.

Working
Away from Home

Working
as a Homemaker

√   1. The salary is $4.25 an hour.   _____

_____   2. It is a full-time job away from home.   _____

_____   3. It is work at home.   _____

_____   4. It is part-time or full-time work at The Market Place.   _____

_____   5. It is a job as a homemaker.   _____

_____   6. It is a job as a cashier.   _____

Exercise 4: Understanding Sounds

A. Directions: Read these.

g + r = *gr* as in <u>gr</u>andmother

b + r = *br* as in <u>br</u>ead

B. Directions: Circle the word with the same sound as the letters underlined.

1. <u>br</u>eakfast   brother   birth

2. <u>gr</u>andmother   girls   grey

3. <u>br</u>other   drive   bread

4. <u>gr</u>ey   hungry   hamburger

Exercise 5: Understanding Language

Directions: Choose the correct word. Write it in the blank.

himself   herself   themselves   myself   yourself

1. The children clean their rooms *themselves* _____ .

2. Raj cooks his breakfast _____ .

3. Mary cooks lunch for _____ and the children.

4. Carmen does all the housework _____ .

5. The children wash the dishes _____ after dinner.

6. I always make my bed _____ in the morning. My mother doesn't help me.

7. You can ride that bicycle _____ . You don't need any help.

8. My father built our house _____ .

WORKING AWAY FROM HOME

Rosalie and David Boone work full-time. They both have to work to earn enough money for their family.

Rosalie works at The Market Place Monday through Friday from 9:00 A.M. to 5:00 P.M. She is a cashier. David is a cook at King's Restaurant. He works at the restaurant Tuesday through Saturday from 7:00 A.M. to 3:00 P.M.

David eats breakfast at the restaurant. He cooks it himself. Before she goes to work, Rosalie eats breakfast at home. She cooks it for herself and their children. After work, David cooks dinner for the family. The family eats dinner together.

After dinner, Rosalie cleans the house and David washes the dishes. The three children clean their rooms themselves and do their homework.

Directions: Read the questions. Find the answers in the narrative. Write the answers.

1. Why do Rosalie and David have to work? _____

_____

2. Where does Rosalie work? _____

_____

3. Where does David work? _____

_____

4. What does David do after work? _____

_____

5. Write two things the children do after dinner? _____

_____

WORKING AS A HOMEMAKER

Stan and Emily Gibbs have two children. Stan is a police officer. He works in the city Monday through Friday from 8:00 A.M. to 4:00 P.M. Emily doesn't go out to work. She works at home every day. She is a homemaker. She does all the work in the house herself. Every morning, she cooks breakfast for her family and cleans the kitchen. When her husband is working and her children are at school, Emily does the housework. She washes the clothes and cleans the house. She also does the grocery shopping herself. Some days she finishes early and visits her friends or watches television. On Wednesdays, she takes a math course at a college. On Thursdays, she goes to the library. Other days, she visits her friends or does her homework.

Emily cooks dinner for the family every day. When Stan comes home from work, the family eats dinner together. After dinner, the children wash the dishes themselves, and Emily and Stan drink coffee and talk.

1. Where does Stan work? _____

_____

2. Where does Emily work? _____

_____

3. Does Emily do all the housework herself? _____

_____

4. Write two things Emily does when her husband is working and

her children are in school. _____

_____

Exercise 6: THINK

Directions: Read the narrative. Answer the questions.

Dennis and Linda Wilson are married. They have three children. Dennis works full-time, but Linda does not work away from home. The Wilson family needs more money for clothes and food. Dennis wants to get a part-time job on Saturday. Linda wants to work, too. Dennis does not want Linda to work. He wants her to say home to clean the house and to take care of the children.

	yes	no
Should Linda stay home?	_____	_____
Should Dennis work on Saturday?	_____	_____
Should Linda work full-time?	_____	_____
Should Linda work part-time?	_____	_____
Should Dennis stay home on Saturdays to clean the house?	_____	_____

FOR SALE

HOUSE FOR SALE

10-year-old house 6 rooms, 3 bedrooms, new kitchen, living room with fireplace, porch, two-car garage, large yard.

Call: 563-1894

OR

FOR RENT

5-room apartment for rent, 3 bedrooms, new carpet in living room. $250 per month includes heat and hot water. Call after 5:00 p.m. 241-8314

Exercise 1: Understanding Words

A. Directions: Look at the picture and write the word.

1. fireplace _____

2. bank _____

3. yard _____

4. carpet _____

5. garage _____

6. lawn _____

7. paint _____

B. Directions: Read the definitions and write the word.

1. money from the bank
   to buy a house   mortgage _____

2. the top of a building   roof   _____

Exercise 2: Understanding Sentences

Directions: Read the sentences. Look at the pictures. Match them. Write
the right number next to each picture. Then copy the sentence.

1. The fireplace is in the living room.
2. Soraya is parking her car in the garage.
3. The children are playing in the yard.
4. Larry and his grandmother are
   walking on the lawn.
5. The carpet looks good.
6. Chou is painting his house.

Exercise 3: Careful Reading

HOUSE FOR SALE

10-year-old house 6 rooms, 3 bedrooms, new kitchen, living room with fireplace, porch, two-car garage, large yard. Call: 563-1894

FOR RENT

5-room apartment for rent, 3 bedrooms, new carpet in living room. $250 per month includes heat and hot water. Call after 5:00 p.m. 241-8314

Directions: Read and check the right answer.

House   Apartment

_____   1. It is 10 years old.   _____

_____   2. It has a new kitchen.   _____

_____   3. It has a new carpet in the   _____
                       living room.

_____   4. It has a fireplace in the   _____
                       living room.

_____   5. It has a two-car garage.   _____

_____   6. It has 3 bedrooms.   _____

Exercise 4: Understanding Sounds

A. Directions: Read these.

$$t + r = tr \text{ as in } \underline{tr}\text{affic} \qquad t + h = th \text{ as in } \underline{th}e$$
$$p + r = pr \text{ as in } \underline{pr}\text{ice}$$

B. Directions: Circle the word with the same sound as the letters underlined.

1. <u>pr</u>ice	parent	prescription
2. ano<u>th</u>er	right	mother
3. bir<u>th</u>	month	tablet
4. <u>th</u>eir	there	take
5. <u>tr</u>affic	three	try

Exercise 5: Understanding Language

Directions: Write the correct form of the verb. Use the present perfect tense. Look at the example.

1. John and Mary *have owned* their house for 11 years.
   (own)

2. John _____ the house two times.
   (paint)

3. The Molinas _____ their roof once.
   (fix)

4. The Chandlers _____ their apartment.
   (rent)

5. Their landlord never _____ the roof.
   (fix)

6. He _____ just _____ the apartment building.
   (paint)

7. He _____ their rent two times.
   (increase)

BUYING

John and Mary Smith own a house. They have owned it for 11 years. Their house has a big yard. John or Mary cuts the lawn every week. They have painted the house two times and have fixed the roof once. Mary and John Smith pay a mortgage to the bank every month. They have paid this mortgage for 11 years. Their mortgage payment is always the same. When John and Mary want to move, they will sell their house.

Directions: Read the questions. Find the answers in the narrative. Write the answers.

1. How long have John and Mary owned their house?

_____

2. Who painted the Smiths' house?

_____

3. Has their mortgage payment increased?   yes   no

4. What will Mary and John do when they want to move?

_____

RENTING

Charles and Diane Chandler rent an apartment. They have rented it for six years. They do not have a yard. The landlord has just painted the apartment building. He has never fixed the roof. Charles and Diane Chandler pay rent to the landlord every month. The landlord can increase the rent. He has increased the Chandlers' rent two times. When Diane and Charles want to move, they will tell their landlord. Then he will rent the apartment to another family.

Directions: Read the questions. Find the answers in the narrative. Write the answers.

1. How long have Diane and Charles rented their apartment?

_____

2. Who painted the apartment building?

_____

3. Has their rent increased?   yes   no

4. What will Charles and Diane do when they want to move?

_____

Exercise 6: THINK

Rita and Pablo Molina saved money for a long time. They wanted to move to a better street. Pablo wanted to buy a house there. He read the newspaper every day. He has just seen an ad for the house he wanted to buy. This house looked beautiful. It had three bedrooms, a new kitchen, a two-car garage, and a fireplace in the living room.

Pablo's wife Rita did not want to buy a house. She wanted to rent another apartment with more rooms. She saw an ad for a 3-bedroom apartment with new carpet in the living room. The rent was only $250 a month.

Pablo wanted to look at the house. Rita wanted to look at the apartment.

	yes	no
1. Should Pablo and Rita buy a house?	_____	_____
2. Should Rita and Pablo rent another apartment?	_____	_____
3. Do you rent an apartment?	_____	_____
4. Do you own a house?	_____	_____
5. Would you like to move to a better street?	_____	_____

Lesson 7 **What to Drive - To Buy a New or Used Car**

USED CAR

7-year-old 4-door sedan, 4 new tires, large trunk, 65,000 miles. For sale by owner. Call 418-5129.

OR

NEW! STATION WAGON

8 passenger, radio and 2 year or 24,000 mile warranty. $6,500. Car City, 128 South Street, open daily from 9-5.

Exercise 1: Understanding Words

Directions: Study the pictures and the words. Write the words.

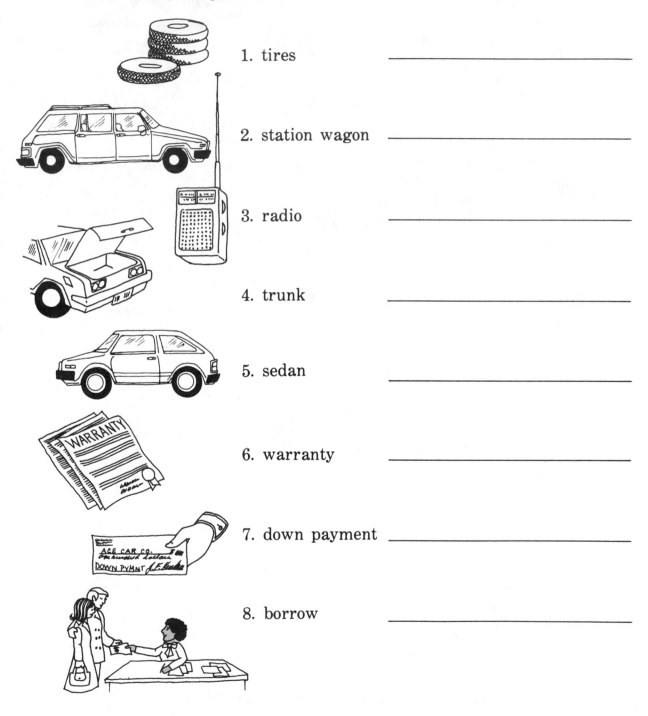

1. tires _____

2. station wagon _____

3. radio _____

4. trunk _____

5. sedan _____

6. warranty _____

7. down payment _____

8. borrow _____

Exercise 2: Understanding Sentences

Directions: Read the sentences. Look at the pictures. Match them. Write
the number next to the right picture. Then copy the sentence.

1. This sedan is new.
2. Eight people can sit in this station wagon.
3. Amir is fixing the flat tire on his car.
4. The car radio sounds good.
5. Kevin doesn't have any room in his trunk.
6. Joan did not have enough money.
   She is borrowing money from the bank.

Exercise 3: Careful Reading

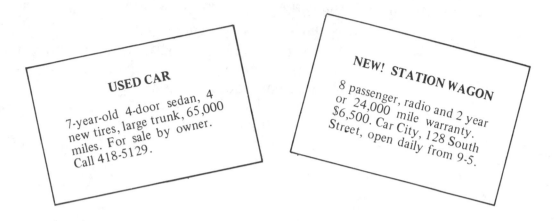

USED CAR

7-year-old 4-door sedan, 4 new tires, large trunk, 65,000 miles. For sale by owner. Call 418-5129.

NEW! STATION WAGON

8 passenger, radio and 2 year or 24,000 mile warranty. $6,500. Car City, 128 South Street, open daily from 9-5.

Directions: Read the page carefully. Then check the right answer.

Used Car   New Car

_____   1. It has room for eight passengers.   _____

_____   2. It has a two-year warranty.   _____

_____   3. This car has four new tires.   _____

_____   4. This car costs $6,500.   _____

_____   5. It is for sale by the owner.   _____

_____   6. It is for sale at Car City.   _____

Exercise 4: Understanding Sounds

A. Read these.

a + i = *ai* as in p<u>ai</u>nt

d + r = *dr* as in <u>dr</u>ink

B. Directions: Circle the word with the same sound as the letters underlined.

1. p<u>ai</u>nt   pass   paid

2. <u>dr</u>ive   dress   dinner

3. p<u>ai</u>d   meat   painting

4. <u>dr</u>ink   driver   directions

Exercise 5: Understanding Language

Directions: Write the correct form of the verb in parentheses. (choose the past tense or the present perfect tense) Look at the examples.

1. They ___*bought*___ the car three months ago.
   (buy)

   They *have just bought* the car.
   (buy)

2. Sam _____ the car seven years. Then he sold it.
   (own)

   The Hupkas _____ the car three months.
   (own)

3. They _____ money from the bank.
   (not borrow)

   They _____ never _____ money from
   the bank.   (borrow)

4. They _____ cash three months ago.
   (pay)

   They _____ just _____ for a new radio.
   (pay)

63

A NEW CAR

Brian and Kate Murphy have just bought a new station wagon at Car City. They have owned it one month. They decided to buy a station wagon because they have three children and a dog. Their new car is blue and grey. It looks beautiful. It has a radio and an extra seat in the back for the children.

This new station wagon cost $6,500. Kate and Brian did not have enough cash for their new car. They had some money for a down payment. They had to borrow some money from the bank. Now they must pay the bank $100 a month for four years. They have borrowed money from the bank before.

Usually new cars do not need repairs. If the Murphys' car needs a new engine or some other new parts, Mr. and Mrs. Murphy will not have to pay for them. Their new car has a two-year warranty. Car City will replace parts for free for two years. They had a problem with their radio last week. Car City has just repaired it for free.

Directions: Read the questions. Find the answers in the narrative. Write the answers.

1. When did Brian and Kate buy the car?

   _____

2. Did Kate and Brian borrow money to buy the car?   yes   no

3. Does the car have a warranty?   yes   no

4. Write two sentences to describe the car.

   _____

   _____

A USED CAR

Wesley Simpson sold his car to his friends Makiko and Kenzi Ogawa three months ago. Now the Ogawas have owned it for three months. It cost $1,500 and they like it.

The car is a 4-door sedan. It's seven years old and looks old. It has a new engine. The Ogawas have just decided to buy a new car radio.

Mr. and Mrs. Ogawa paid cash for this car. They did not borrow money from the bank. They didn't want to borrow money from the bank. They have never borrowed money for a car.

Sometimes used cars need repairs. When their car needs repairs, Mr. and Mrs. Ogawa must pay the bills. Their used car doesn't have a warranty. They have just paid $67.00 for a car repair.

Directions: Read the questions. Find the answers in the narrative. Write the answers.

1. When did Makiko and Kenzi buy the car?

_____

2. How much did the car cost?

_____

3. Did Kenzi and Makiko borrow money to buy the car?   yes   no

4. Does the car have a warranty?   yes   no

5. Write two sentences to describe the car.

_____

_____

Exercise 6: THINK

Directions: This is the warranty for Mr. and Mrs. Murphy's new car. Read it carefully and answer the questions.

WARRANTY

This car has a 24-month warranty. Car City will replace any defective parts. Return the car to Car City. Car City will replace the defective parts at no cost to the owner.

---

1. Brian and Kate Murphy bought their car in January 1981. In January 1982 it doesn't work. Will Car City repair their car? _____

2. Mr. and Mrs. Murphy's car needs repairs. Where will they take it? _____

3. Will Car City replace the parts for free?

   _____

4. Kate and Brian bought their car in January 1981. When will the warranty end? _____

Check-Up   Unit Two: Lessons 5-7

Exercise 1: Understanding Sounds

Directions: Circle the word with the same sound as the letters underlined.

1. grey   hungry   hamburger
2. another   right   mother
3. price   parent   prescription
4. brother   bread   birth

Exercise 2: Understanding Sentences

Directions: Write the right sentence next to each picture.

The children are playing in the yard.
The fireplace is in the living room.
Amir is fixing the flat tire on his car.
Kevin doesn't have any room in his trunk.

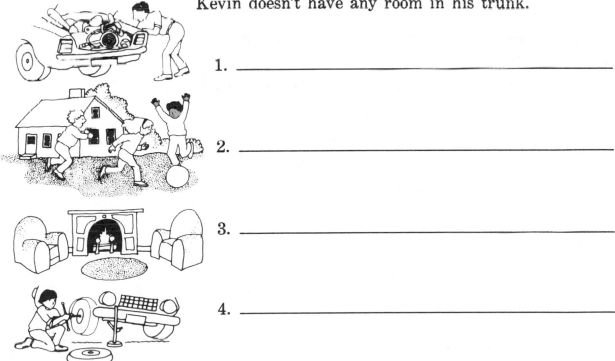

1. _____

2. _____

3. _____

4. _____

Exercise 3: Careful Reading

Directions: Read the ads and check the right answers.

A.

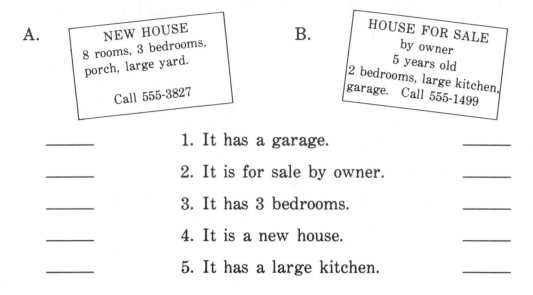

NEW HOUSE
8 rooms, 3 bedrooms,
porch, large yard.

Call 555-3827

B.

HOUSE FOR SALE
by owner
5 years old
2 bedrooms, large kitchen,
garage. Call 555-1499

_____   1. It has a garage.   _____

_____   2. It is for sale by owner.   _____

_____   3. It has 3 bedrooms.   _____

_____   4. It is a new house.   _____

_____   5. It has a large kitchen.   _____

Exercise 4: Understanding Paragraphs

A. Read these two paragraphs about renting and buying.

    Joel and Jan rent an apartment in the city. They have
rented it for three years. They do not have a yard.
    Joel wants to buy a house. He likes to work in the yard.
He wants to plant a garden.

B. Directions: Read the questions. Find the answers in the narrative.
Then write the answers.

1. How long have Jan and Joel rented an apartment?

_____

2. What does Joel want to buy?

_____

3. Where does he like to work?

_____

UNIT THREE
Consumer Choices

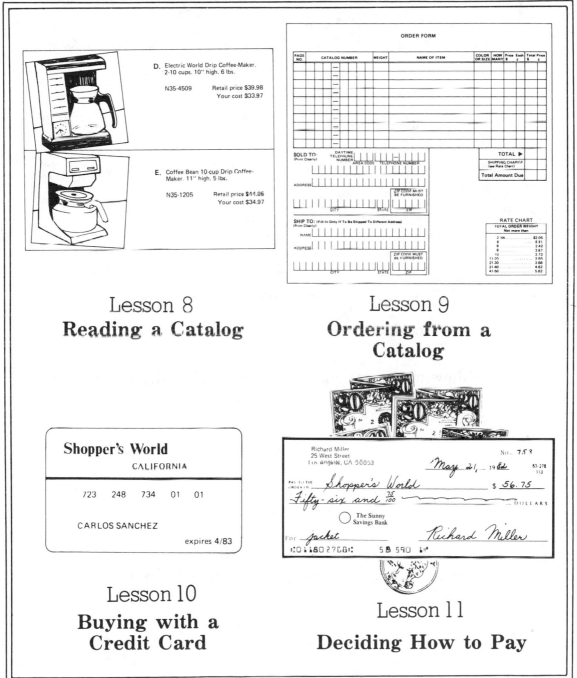

D. Electric World Drip Coffee-Maker.
2-10 cups. 10" high. 6 lbs.

N35-4509   Retail price $39.98
Your cost $33.97

E. Coffee Bean 10-cup Drip Coffee-Maker. 11" high. 5 lbs.

N35-1205   Retail price $44.06
Your cost $34.97

Lesson 8
Reading a Catalog

Lesson 9
Ordering from a Catalog

Shopper's World
CALIFORNIA

723   248   734   01   01

CARLOS SANCHEZ

expires 4/83

Richard Miller
25 West Street
Los Angeles, CA 00003

No. 753

May 21, 1982

PAY TO THE ORDER OF   Shopper's World $ 56.75

Fifty-six and 75/100   DOLLARS

The Sunny Savings Bank

For jacket   Richard Miller

Lesson 10
Buying with a Credit Card

Lesson 11
Deciding How to Pay

Student Reading Objectives

1. to recognize and read the following letter combinations: *pl, bl, wr, cr, sm, sp, sc, sk, ph, sn, sl*
2. to understand the denotative meaning of catalogs, credit cards, and credit card statements
3. to recall specific information
4. to understand the meaning of relevant vocabulary by using definition clues
5. to understand the meaning of relevant vocabulary by using summary clues
6. to make generalizations
7. to draw conclusions

ESL Information

The following intermediate-level grammatical structures are used and practiced for the first time in Unit Three.

1. comparison of nouns: more, less, fewer, as many _____ as, as much _____ as
2. negative imperatives: (*Don't* shout!)
3. possessive pronouns: *mine, yours, his, hers, ours, theirs*

A review of the simple present tense, the present continuous tense, the simple past tense, and the present perfect tense also appears in this Unit.

Lesson 8 Reading a Catalog

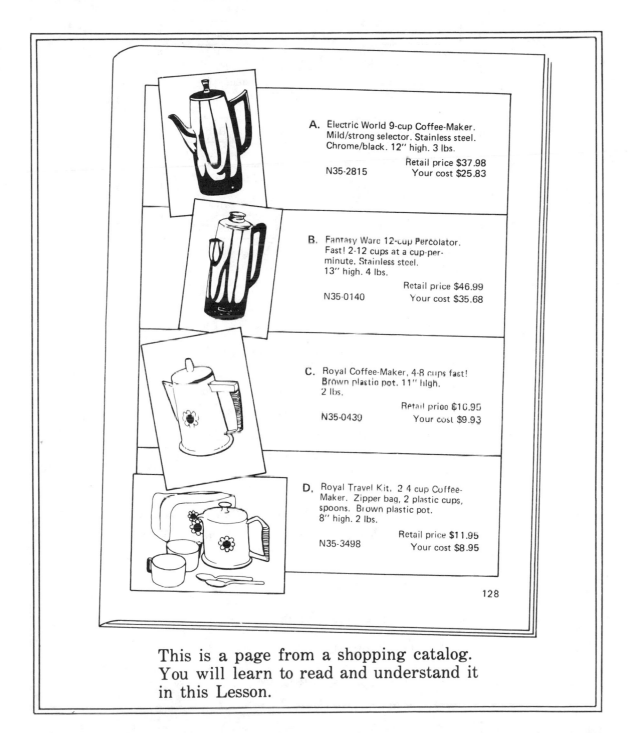

A. Electric World 9-cup Coffee-Maker. Mild/strong selector. Stainless steel. Chrome/black. 12" high. 3 lbs.

N35-2815 Retail price $37.98
Your cost $25.83

B. Fantasy Ware 12-cup Percolator. Fast! 2-12 cups at a cup-per-minute. Stainless steel. 13" high. 4 lbs.

N35-0140 Retail price $46.99
Your cost $35.68

C. Royal Coffee-Maker, 4-8 cups fast! Brown plastic pot. 11" high. 2 lbs.

N35-0439 Retail price $16.95
Your cost $9.93

D. Royal Travel Kit. 2-4 cup Coffee-Maker. Zipper bag, 2 plastic cups, spoons. Brown plastic pot. 8" high. 2 lbs.

N35-3498 Retail price $11.95
Your cost $8.95

128

This is a page from a shopping catalog. You will learn to read and understand it in this Lesson.

Understanding Catalogs

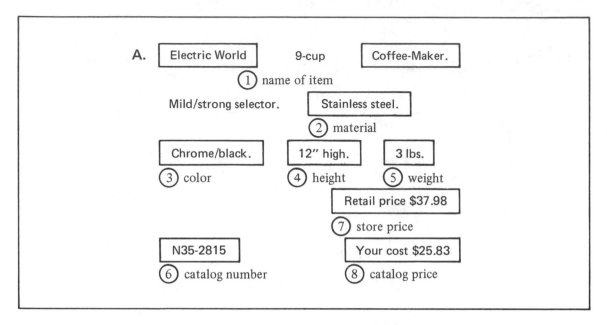

1. It is a coffee-maker.
2. It is made of stainless steel.
3. It is chrome and black.
4. It is twelve-inches high.
5. It weighs three pounds.
6. Its catalog number is N35-2815.
7. It costs $37.98 in a store.
8. It costs $25.83 from a catalog.

Directions: Look at the catalog ad for the coffee-maker. Write the right number.

1. _____ It's the height.

2. _____ It's the catalog price.

3. _____ It's the weight.

4. _____ It's the catalog number.

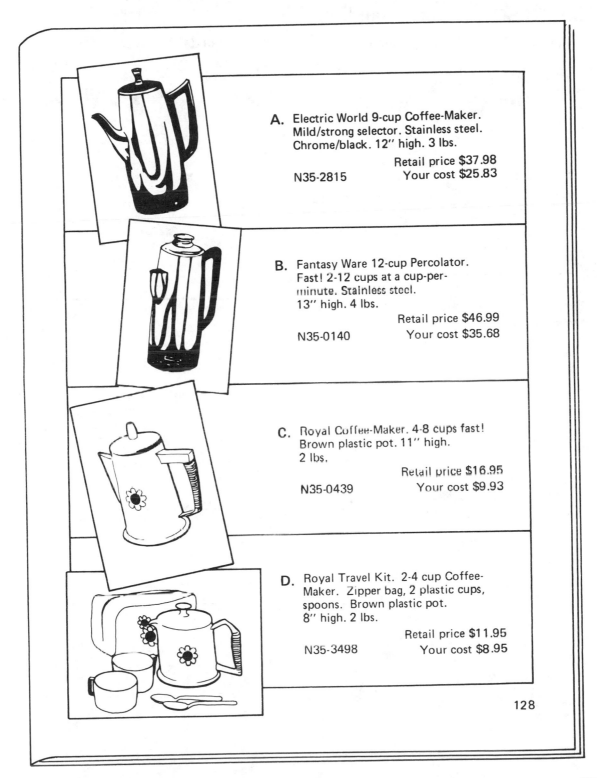

A. Electric World 9-cup Coffee-Maker. Mild/strong selector. Stainless steel. Chrome/black. 12" high. 3 lbs.

N35-2815

Retail price $37.98
Your cost $25.83

B. Fantasy Ware 12-cup Percolator. Fast! 2-12 cups at a cup-per-minute. Stainless steel. 13" high. 4 lbs.

N35-0140

Retail price $46.99
Your cost $35.68

C. Royal Coffee-Maker. 4-8 cups fast! Brown plastic pot. 11" high. 2 lbs.

N35-0439

Retail price $16.95
Your cost $9.93

D. Royal Travel Kit. 2-4 cup Coffee-Maker. Zipper bag, 2 plastic cups, spoons. Brown plastic pot. 8" high. 2 lbs.

N35-3498

Retail price $11.95
Your cost $8.95

128

Exercise 1: Understanding Words

Directions: Look at the picture. Read the word or words. Write the word or words.

1. cup   _____

2. coffee-maker   _____

   percolator   _____

3. "   _____

   inch   _____

4. lbs.   _____

   pounds   _____

5. catalog   _____

6. zipper   _____

7. spoon   _____

Exercise 2: Careful Reading

Directions: Read the items from the catalog. Answer the questions.

A. Electric World 9-cup Coffee-Maker.
Mild/strong selector.
Chrome/black. 12" high. 3 lbs.

N35-2815   Retail price $37.98
          Your cost $25.83

B. Fantasy Ware 12-cup Percolator.
Fast! 2-12 cups at a cup-per-
minute. Stainless steel.
13" high. 4 lbs.

N35-0140   Retail price $46.99
          Your cost $35.68

C. Royal Coffee-Maker. 4-8 cups fast!
Brown plastic pot. 11" high.
2 lbs.

N35-0439   Retail price $16.95
          Your cost $9.93

1. Which coffee-maker is made of stainless steel?   A   B   C

2. Which coffee-maker is made of plastic?   A   B   C

3. Who makes coffee-maker A? _____

4. What color is coffee-maker C? _____

5. How much does percolator B cost? _____

6. What is the catalog number for coffee-maker A? _____

7. What is the catalog number for percolator B? _____

Exercise 3: Deciding

CATALOG SHOPPING

Many people like catalog shopping. They shop at home and use less gas in their cars. They also use less time to shop and have more time to relax. And they say items are cheaper in catalogs than in stores.

Other people don't like catalog shopping. They like to shop in stores instead. They say that catalogs don't have as many brands as stores. They also say that items in catalogs cost as much as items in stores.

Directions: Read the narrative. Then read the sentences. Circle the right answer.

1. Everybody likes catalog shopping.   yes   no

2. Everybody likes shopping in stores.   yes   no

3. People have different ideas about shopping.   yes   no

4. Do you like catalog shopping?   yes   no

5. Do you like shopping in stores?   yes   no

6. Which kind of shopping do you like better?   store   catalog

Exercise 4: Understanding Sounds

A. Directions: Read these.

p + l = *pl* as in p<u>l</u>ease

b + l = *bl* as in <u>bl</u>ock

B. Directions: Circle the word with the same sound as the letters underlined.

1. p<u>l</u>ease   apartment   playing

2. <u>bl</u>ouse   black   behind

3. firep<u>l</u>ace   parking   apple

4. <u>bl</u>ue   block   bill

5. plastic   police   please

Exercise 5: Understanding Language

Directions: Read the sentences. Choose the right answer. Write it.

1. I work all the time. I need _____ time to relax.
   more/less

2. My neighbor drives his car 60 miles every day. I only drive my car 20 miles every Saturday. I use _____ gas than my neighbor.
   more/less

3. My brother has four cats. I have two cats. I have _____ cats than my brother.
   more/fewer

4. Our family has two cars. Our neighbors have two cars. We have _____ cars as our neighbors.
   as many/more/fewer

5. The catalog sells four percolators. Our store sells eight percolators. The catalog sells _____ percolators than our store.
   more/fewer

Exercise 6: THINK

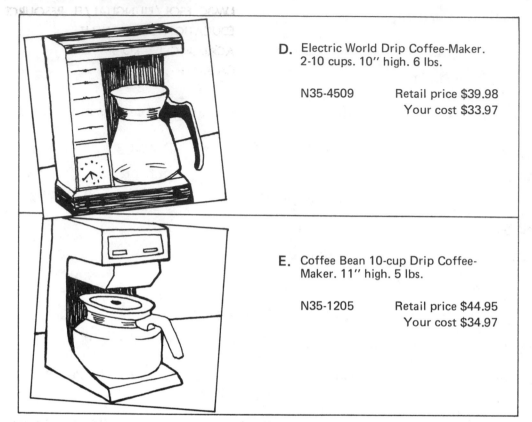

D. Electric World Drip Coffee-Maker. 2-10 cups. 10″ high. 6 lbs.

N35-4509   Retail price $39.98
            Your cost $33.97

E. Coffee Bean 10-cup Drip Coffee-Maker. 11″ high. 5 lbs.

N35-1205   Retail price $44.95
            Your cost $34.97

Directions: Read about the two coffee-makers. Then read the sentences below and circle yes or no.

1. **D** costs less than **E**.   yes   no

2. **D** makes more cups than **E**.   yes   no

3. **E** makes fewer cups than **D**.   yes   no

4. **D** makes as many cups as **E**.   yes   no

5. **E** costs as much as **D**.   yes   no

6. **E** is shorter than **D**.   yes   no

7. **D** is as high as **E**.   yes   no

Lesson 9 Ordering from a Catalog

ORDER FORM

PAGE NO.	CATALOG NUMBER	WEIGHT	NAME OF ITEM	COLOR OR SIZE	HOW MANY	Price Each $ ¢	Total Price $ ¢
	—						
	—						
	—						
	—						
	—						
	—						
	—						
	—						
	—						
	—						

SOLD TO:
(Print Clearly)

DAYTIME TELEPHONE NUMBER
AREA CODE   TELEPHONE NUMBER

ADDRESS

CITY   STATE   ZIP
ZIP CODE MUST BE FURNISHED

SHIP TO: (Fill In Only If To Be Shipped To Different Address)
(Print Clearly)

NAME

ADDRESS

CITY   STATE   ZIP
ZIP CODE MUST BE FURNISHED

TOTAL ▶

SHIPPING CHARGE (See Rate Chart)

Total Amount Due

RATE CHART

TOTAL ORDER WEIGHT Not more than	
2 lbs.	$2.05
4	2.21
6	2.42
8	2.57
10	2.73
11-20	3.05
21-30	3.68
31-40	4.62
41-50	5.62

This is an order form from a catalog.
You will learn how to fill it out in this
Lesson.

D. Royal Travel Kit. 2-4 cup Coffee-
Maker. Zipper bag, 2 plastic cups,
spoons. Brown plastic pot.
8″ high. 2 lbs.

N35-3498

Retail price $11.95
Your cost $8.95

① ——————————→ 280

① The Royal Travel Kit is advertised on page 280.

② Its catalog number is N35-3498.

③ It weighs two pounds.

④ Mary Lewis wants to order one Royal Travel Kit.

⑤ Each Royal Travel Kit costs $8.95.

⑥ One Royal Travel Kit doesn't weigh more than two pounds.
The shipping charge is $2.05.

⑦ Mary Lewis must pay a total of $11.00.

⑧ Mary Lewis is buying the Royal Travel Kit for John Lewis.

Directions: Look at the catalog ad for the travel kit. Write the right number.

1. _____ It's the total Mary must pay.

2. _____ It's the shipping charge.

3. _____ It's the page number.

4. _____ It's the weight.

ORDER FORM

PAGE NO.	CATALOG NUMBER								WEIGHT	NAME OF ITEM	COLOR OR SIZE	HOW MANY	Price Each $	¢	Total Price $	¢
280	N	3	5	—	3	4	9	8	2	Royal Travel Kit	—	1	8	95	8	95
				—												
				—												
				—												
				—												
				—												
				—												
				—												
				—												
				—												

SOLD TO: (Print Clearly)

DAYTIME TELEPHONE NUMBER: 6 1 7 555 − 8 0 8 8
AREA CODE — TELEPHONE NUMBER

M A R Y   L E W I S

ADDRESS 7 5   L O R D   S T R E E T

B O S T O N | M A   0 2 1 1 5
CITY   STATE   ZIP

ZIP CODE MUST BE FURNISHED

SHIP TO: (Fill In Only If To Be Shipped To Different Address) (Print Clearly)

NAME J O H N   L E W I S

ADDRESS 5 2   A V A L O N   S T R E E T

C L E V E L A N D   O H   4 4 1 1 6
CITY   STATE   ZIP

ZIP CODE MUST BE FURNISHED

TOTAL ▶	8 95
SHIPPING CHARGE (see Rate Chart)	2 05
Total Amount Due	11 00

RATE CHART

TOTAL ORDER WEIGHT
Not more than

2 lbs.	$2.06
4	2.21
6	2.42
8	2.57
10	2.73
11-20	3.05
21-30	3.68
31-40	4.62
41-50	5.62

Circled numbers: ② ③ ④ ⑤ ⑥ ⑦ ⑧

Exercise 1: Understanding Words

Directions: Look at the picture. Read the word or words. Write the word or words.

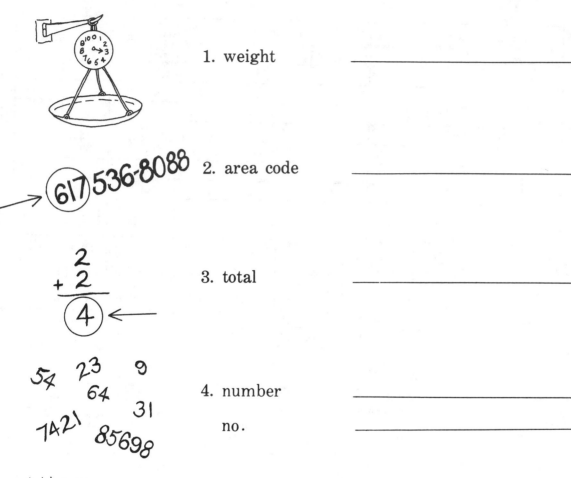

1. weight _____

2. area code _____

3. total _____

4. number _____

   no. _____

5. zip code _____

6. shipping charge _____

Exercise 2: Careful Reading

Directions: Read the item from the catalog. Answer the questions.

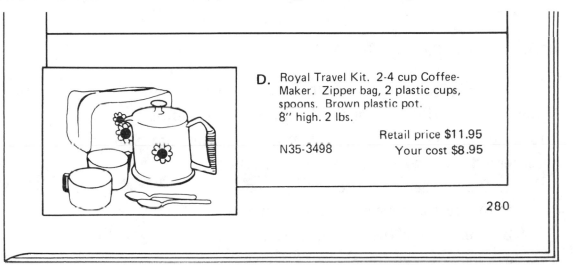

D. Royal Travel Kit. 2-4 cup Coffee-Maker. Zipper bag, 2 plastic cups, spoons. Brown plastic pot. 8″ high. 2 lbs.

N35-3498

Retail price $11.95
Your cost $8.95

280

1. The Royal Travel Kit is on page 281.   yes   no

2. Its weight is two pounds.   yes   no

3. The Royal Travel Kit weighs more than two pounds.   yes   no

4. What is the Royal Travel Kit's catalog number? _____

5. What is the catalog cost for the Royal Travel Kit? _____

6. How high is the Royal Travel Kit? _____

Exercise 3: Deciding

Directions: Read the narrative. Answer the questions.

ORDERING FROM A CATALOG

It takes a lot of time to fill out a catalog order form correctly. When you're filling it out, you have to be careful. You have to read and write carefully. You have to read the rate chart correctly. Here are some other suggestions.

1. Remember to write the zip codes.
2. Write the correct page number.
3. Don't write the wrong area code.
4. Don't forget the shipping charge.

Directions: Read the sentences. Circle the right answer.

1. Zip codes are important.	yes	no
2. The shipping charge is important.	yes	no
3. It is easy to fill out a catalog order form correctly.	yes	no
4. Many people write the wrong area code.	yes	no
5. Have you ever filled out a catalog order form?	yes	no

Exercise 4: Understanding Sounds

A. Directions: Read these.

    w + r = *wr* as in <u>wr</u>ite   c + r = *cr* as in a<u>cr</u>oss

               s + m = *sm* as in <u>sm</u>all

B. Directions: Circle the word with the same sound as the letters underlined.

1. <u>wr</u>ite	waitress	wrong
2. a<u>cr</u>oss	secretary	correct
3. <u>wr</u>ote	word	writing
4. <u>sm</u>all	Sam	Smith

Exercise 5: Understanding Language

Directions: Change these commands to the negative. Read the example first.

Example: Walk slowly!
        <u>Don't walk slowly!</u>

1. Write with a pen!

_____

2. Order from a catalog!

_____

3. Use my car!

_____

4. Eat this apple!

_____

5. Close the door!

_____

6. Open the door!

_____

7. Turn off the radio!

_____

Exercise 6: THINK

Directions: You want to order item E, the Coffee Bean Coffee-Maker. Fill
out the order form below.

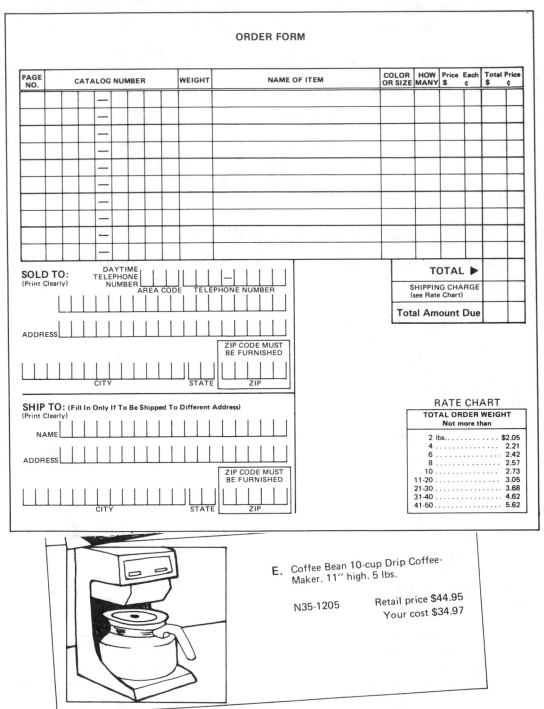

ORDER FORM

PAGE NO.	CATALOG NUMBER	WEIGHT	NAME OF ITEM	COLOR OR SIZE	HOW MANY	Price Each $ ¢	Total Price $ ¢
	—						
	—						
	—						
	—						
	—						
	—						
	—						
	—						
	—						
	—						

SOLD TO: (Print Clearly)

DAYTIME TELEPHONE NUMBER
AREA CODE — TELEPHONE NUMBER

ADDRESS

CITY   STATE   ZIP

ZIP CODE MUST BE FURNISHED

TOTAL ▶

SHIPPING CHARGE (see Rate Chart)

Total Amount Due

SHIP TO: (Fill In Only If To Be Shipped To Different Address)
(Print Clearly)

NAME

ADDRESS

CITY   STATE   ZIP

ZIP CODE MUST BE FURNISHED

RATE CHART

TOTAL ORDER WEIGHT Not more than	
2 lbs.	$2.05
4	2.21
6	2.42
8	2.57
10	2.73
11-20	3.05
21-30	3.68
31-40	4.62
41-50	5.62

E. Coffee Bean 10-cup Drip Coffee-Maker. 11″ high. 5 lbs.

N35-1205   Retail price $44.95
Your cost $34.97

Lesson 10 Buying with a Credit Card

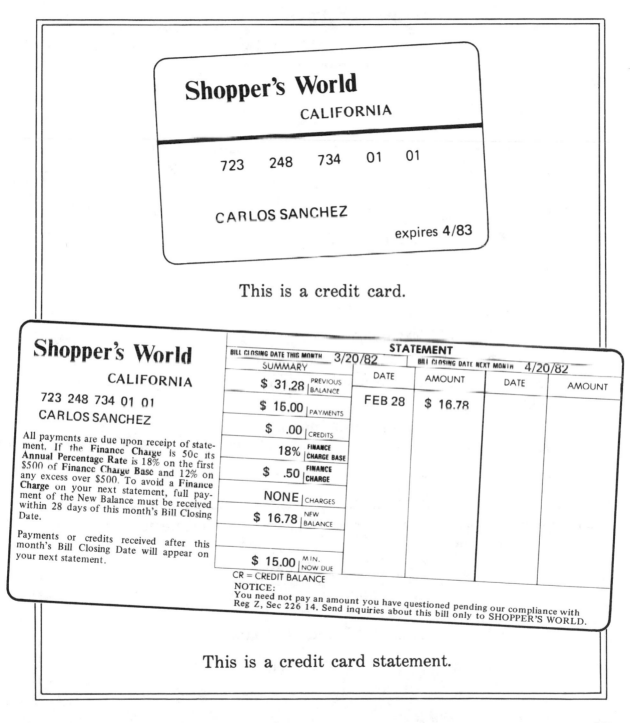

Shopper's World
CALIFORNIA

723   248   734   01   01

CARLOS SANCHEZ

expires 4/83

This is a credit card.

Shopper's World
CALIFORNIA

723 248 734 01 01

CARLOS SANCHEZ

All payments are due upon receipt of statement. If the **Finance Charge** is 50c its **Annual Percentage Rate** is 18% on the first $500 of **Finance Charge Base** and 12% on any excess over $500. To avoid a **Finance Charge** on your next statement, full payment of the New Balance must be received within 28 days of this month's Bill Closing Date.

Payments or credits received after this month's Bill Closing Date will appear on your next statement.

STATEMENT

BILL CLOSING DATE THIS MONTH 3/20/82

BILL CLOSING DATE NEXT MONTH 4/20/82

SUMMARY

$ 31.28	PREVIOUS BALANCE
$ 16.00	PAYMENTS
$ .00	CREDITS
18%	FINANCE CHARGE BASE
$ .50	FINANCE CHARGE
NONE	CHARGES
$ 16.78	NEW BALANCE
$ 15.00	MIN. NOW DUE

DATE	AMOUNT	DATE	AMOUNT
FEB 28	$ 16.78		

CR = CREDIT BALANCE

NOTICE:
You need not pay an amount you have questioned pending our compliance with Reg Z, Sec 226 14. Send inquiries about this bill only to SHOPPER'S WORLD.

This is a credit card statement.

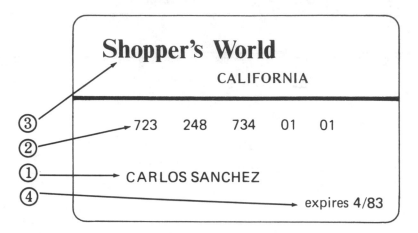

① This is Carlos Sanchez's credit card.

② His credit card number is 7232487340101.

③ He has a credit card at Shopper's World.

④ He can't use this card after April 1983.

⑤ He owed $31.28 last month.

⑥ He paid $15.00 last month.

⑦ He didn't return anything last month.

⑧ He owes $.50 more because he didn't pay the total $31.28 last month.

⑨ He didn't buy anything this month.

⑩ Now he owes $16.78.

⑪ He cannot pay less than $15.00.

Directions: Look at the credit card and the credit card statement. Write the right number.

1. _____ It's the expiration date.

2. _____ It's the name of the store.

3. _____ It's the new balance.

4. _____ It's the finance charge.

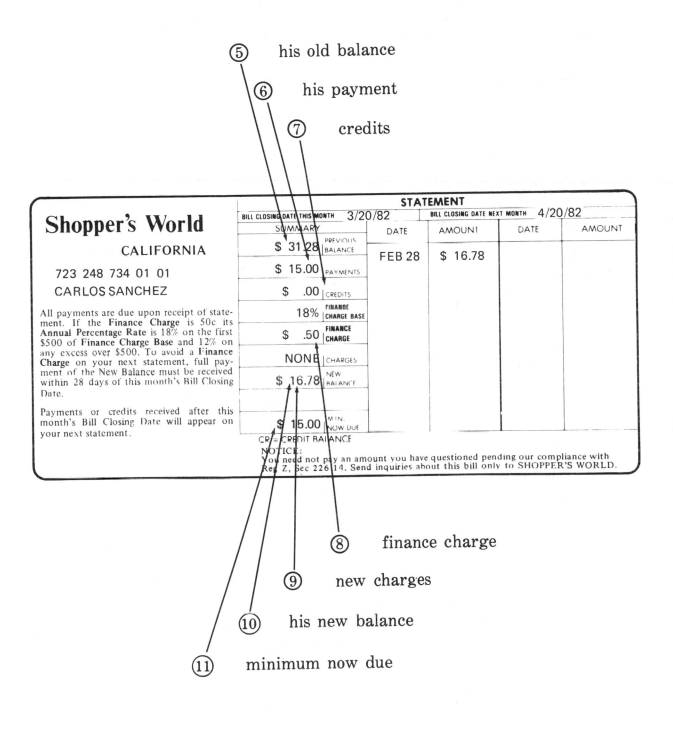

⑤ his old balance

⑥ his payment

⑦ credits

STATEMENT

BILL CLOSING DATE THIS MONTH	3/20/82		BILL CLOSING DATE NEXT MONTH	4/20/82	
SUMMARY		DATE	AMOUNT	DATE	AMOUNT
$ 31.28 PREVIOUS BALANCE		FEB 28	$ 16.78		
$ 15.00 PAYMENTS					
$ .00 CREDITS					
18% FINANCE CHARGE BASE					
$ .50 FINANCE CHARGE					
NONE CHARGES					
$ 16.78 NEW BALANCE					
$ 15.00 MIN. NOW DUE					

Shopper's World
CALIFORNIA

723 248 734 01 01

CARLOS SANCHEZ

All payments are due upon receipt of statement. If the **Finance Charge** is 50c its **Annual Percentage Rate** is 18% on the first $500 of **Finance Charge Base** and 12% on any excess over $500. To avoid a **Finance Charge** on your next statement, full payment of the New Balance must be received within 28 days of this month's Bill Closing Date.

Payments or credits received after this month's Bill Closing Date will appear on your next statement.

CR = CREDIT BALANCE

NOTICE:
You need not pay an amount you have questioned pending our compliance with Reg Z, Sec 226.14. Send inquiries about this bill only to SHOPPER'S WORLD.

⑧ finance charge

⑨ new charges

⑩ his new balance

⑪ minimum now due

89

Exercise 1: Understanding Words

Directions: Look at the picture. Read the word or words. Write the word
or words.

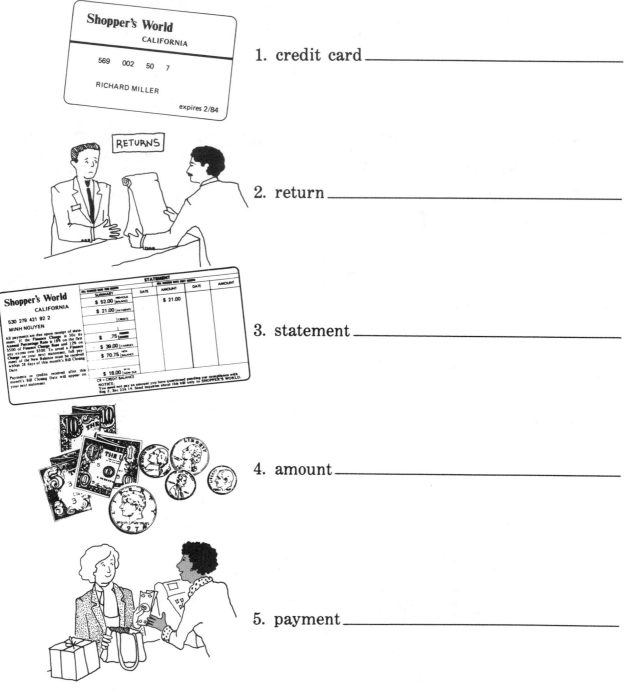

1. credit card _____

2. return _____

3. statement _____

4. amount _____

5. payment _____

Exercise 2: Careful Reading

Directions: Read the credit card statement. Answer the questions.

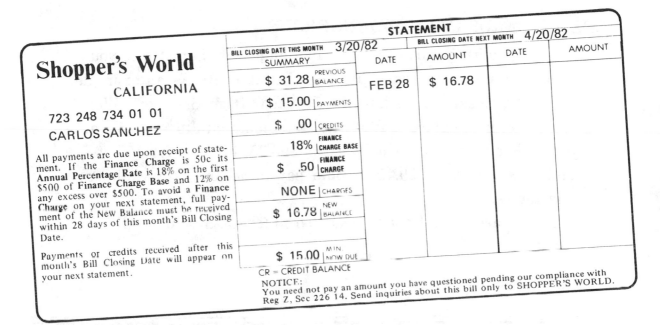

1. This is a credit card.	yes	no
2. Carlos Sanchez owed $31.28 last month.	yes	no
3. Carlos Sanchez paid $.50 last month.	yes	no
4. He spent $16.78 this month.	yes	no
5. How much did he pay last month?	_____	
6. How much does he have to pay this month?	_____	
7. Did he return anything last month?	_____	
8. What is his credit card number?	_____	

Exercise 3: Deciding

Directions: Read the narrative. Answer the questions.

CREDIT CARDS CAN BE DANGEROUS

Buying with credit cards can be dangerous. Sometimes you spend too much and can't pay the bill later. Here's an example.

Robert, Susan, and I have credit cards from Shopper's World. Last month the store mailed the statements on July 20. We got our bills on July 22. Mine was for $50.95, his was for $75.50, and hers was for $129.40. I could pay mine, but they couldn't pay theirs.

So be careful and don't spend too much with your credit cards.

1. How much did Robert spend? _____

2. How much did Susan spend? _____

3. When did the store mail the statements? _____

4. Susan and Robert didn't have enough money to pay their
   bills.   yes   no

5. Credit cards are dangerous for everybody.   yes   no

6. Do you have a credit card?   yes   no

Exercise 4: Understanding Sounds

A. Directions: Read these.

    s + p = *sp* as in s<u>p</u>end

    s + k = *sk* as in <u>sk</u>irt

B. Directions: Circle the word with the same sound as the letters underlined.

1. s<u>p</u>end	speak	soup
2. de<u>sk</u>	ask	dress
3. <u>sk</u>irt	dash	skill
4. <u>sp</u>eak	special	stop

Exercise 5: Understanding Language

Directions: Choose the correct word. Write it in the blank.

mine	yours	his
hers	ours	theirs

1. That car belongs to me. It's _____ .

2. That house belongs to my parents. It's _____ .

3. This pen belongs to my brother. It's _____ .

4. This credit card belongs to you. It's _____ .

5. That dog belongs to us. It's _____ .

6. That sweater belongs to Nita. It's _____ .

7. This percolator belongs to Jim and Lan. It's _____ .

8. That jacket belongs to George. It's _____ .

Exercise 6: THINK

Directions: Read the credit card statement below. Then answer the questions.

STATEMENT

Shopper's World
CALIFORNIA

530 279 421 92 2

MINH NGUYEN

All payments are due upon receipt of statement. If the **Finance Charge** is 50c its **Annual Percentage Rate** is 18% on the first $500 of **Finance Charge Base** and 12% on any excess over $500. To avoid a **Finance Charge** on your next statement, full payment of the New Balance must be received within 28 days of this month's Bill Closing Date.

Payments or credits received after this month's Bill Closing Date will appear on your next statement.

BILL CLOSING DATE THIS MONTH		BILL CLOSING DATE NEXT MONTH		
SUMMARY	DATE	AMOUNT	DATE	AMOUNT
$ 52.00 PREVIOUS BALANCE		$ 21.00		
$ 21.00 PAYMENTS				
CREDITS				
$ .75 FINANCE CHARGE				
$ 39.00 CHARGES				
$ 70.75 NEW BALANCE				
$ 18.00 MIN. NOW DUE				

CR = CREDIT BALANCE

NOTICE:
You need not pay an amount you have questioned pending our compliance with Reg Z, Sec 226 14. Send inquiries about this bill only to SHOPPER'S WORLD.

1. Whose credit card statement is this? _____

2. What is the credit card number? _____

3. How much did she pay last month? _____

4. How much did she buy this month? _____

5. How much does she owe now? _____

6. Does she owe more this month than last month?   yes   no

Lesson 11 Deciding How to Pay

Richard Miller
25 West Street
Los Angeles, CA 90053

No. 753

63-278
113

May 21, 1982

PAY TO THE
ORDER OF Shopper's World $ 56.75

Fifty-six and 75/100 — — — — — — DOLLARS

The Sunny
Savings Bank

Richard Miller

For   jacket

⑈0118027681⑈   5⑈ 590 1⑈

Shopper's World

CALIFORNIA

569   002   50   7

RICHARD MILLER

expires 2/84

These are three ways to pay. You will
learn more about them in this Lesson.

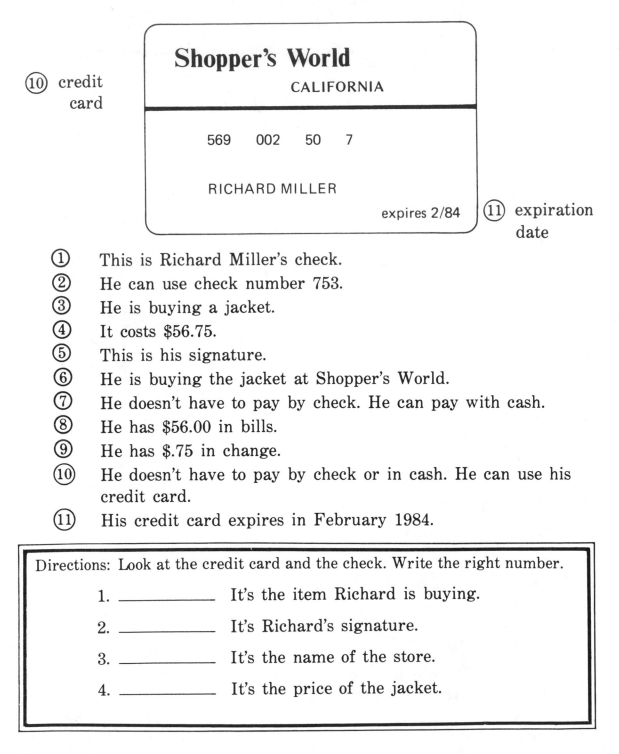

⑩ credit card

Shopper's World

CALIFORNIA

569   002   50   7

RICHARD MILLER

expires 2/84

⑪ expiration date

① This is Richard Miller's check.
② He can use check number 753.
③ He is buying a jacket.
④ It costs $56.75.
⑤ This is his signature.
⑥ He is buying the jacket at Shopper's World.
⑦ He doesn't have to pay by check. He can pay with cash.
⑧ He has $56.00 in bills.
⑨ He has $.75 in change.
⑩ He doesn't have to pay by check or in cash. He can use his credit card.
⑪ His credit card expires in February 1984.

Directions: Look at the credit card and the check. Write the right number.

1. _____ It's the item Richard is buying.

2. _____ It's Richard's signature.

3. _____ It's the name of the store.

4. _____ It's the price of the jacket.

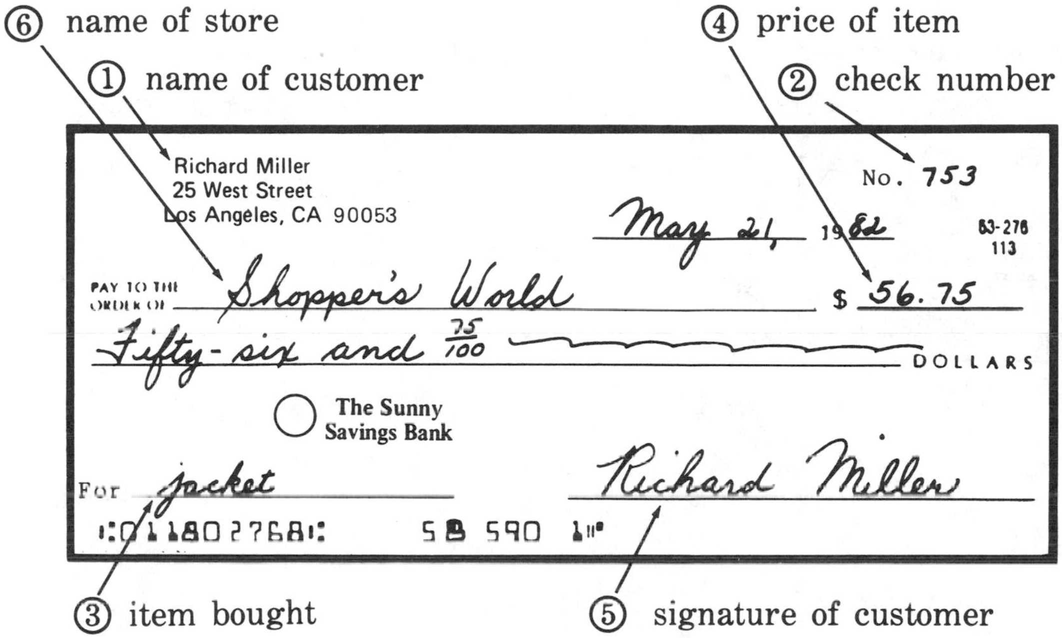

⑥ name of store

④ price of item

① name of customer

② check number

Richard Miller
25 West Street
Los Angeles, CA 90053

No. *753*

May 21, 19*82*

63-276
113

PAY TO THE
ORDER OF *Shopper's World*

$ *56.75*

Fifty-six and $\frac{75}{100}$ ———————————— DOLLARS

The Sunny
Savings Bank

For *jacket*

Richard Miller

⑆011802768⑆   5 8 590 1⁖

③ item bought

⑤ signature of customer

⑧ bills

⑦ cash

⑨ change

Exercise 1: Understanding Words

Directions: Look at the pictures. Read the words. Write the words.

1. customer _____

SIGN HERE *Richard Miller*

2. signature _____

3. bills _____

4. change _____

Exercise 2: Careful Reading

Directions: Look at the check, cash, and credit card again. Answer the questions.

1. The name of the store is Richard Miller. yes no

2. Richard is buying a jacket. yes no

3. Richard's signature is at the bottom of the check. yes no

4. Richard has $56.00 in change. yes no

5. His credit card expires in February 1984. yes no

6. Richard lives in California. yes no

7. Richard wrote 752 checks before this check. yes no

8. The jacket costs $55.70 yes no

9. Richard can pay in three different ways. yes no

10. The credit card is from the Sunny Savings Bank. yes no

Exercise 3: Deciding

Directions: Read the narrative. Answer the questions.

DIFFERENT WAYS TO BUY

Maria, Barry, and Lee work together. Maria is a doctor, Barry is her nurse and Lee is the receptionist. Lee answers the phone and greets patients.

Maria earns a lot of money and has many credit cards. She uses them often. She prefers credit cards to cash because they are safer. She prefers them to checks because they are easier. Maria can get a lot of credit cards because she earns a lot.

Barry and Lee earn less money than Maria, and they have fewer credit cards. They don't use them as much as Maria. They prefer cash and checks. They don't want to spend more than they earn.

1. Who is a receptionist? _____

2. A receptionist answers the phone and greets people.　　　　　　　　　　　　　　　yes　　no

3. Maria can get a lot of credit cards because she earns a lot of money.　　　　　　　　　yes　　no

4. Barry and Lee have fewer credit cards because they earn less money than Maria.　　　　yes　　no

5. Barry and Lee prefer cash to credit cards.　　yes　　no

6. Maria earns more than Lee.　　　　　　　　　yes　　no

Exercise 4: Understanding Sounds

A. Directions: Read these.

p + h = *ph* as in <u>ph</u>one

s + l = *sl* as in <u>sl</u>eep

B. Directions: Circle the word with the same sound as the letters underlined.

1.	<u>sl</u>eep	slow	stop
2.	<u>ph</u>one	please	telephone
3.	<u>sl</u>ow	slacks	skirt
4.	<u>sl</u>eepy	slowly	stove

Exercise 5: Understanding Language

Directions: Choose the right verb. Write it in the blank.

1. Maria usually _____ to buy with credit cards.
   is preferring/prefers

2. Richard _____ a jacket now.
   is buying/buys/bought

3. His jacket _____ $56.75 today.
   is costing/costs/cost

4. Richard's credit card _____ in February 1984.
   is expiring/expires/expired

5. I _____ my credit card for three years.
   am using/use/have used

6. I _____ a dress yesterday with cash.
   am buying/bought/have bought

7. My mother never _____ with a check.
   is paying/pays

8. My father _____ a credit card since 1975.
   is having/has/has had

Exercise 6: THINK

HOW DO YOU PAY?

A. Directions: This exercise is about you. Read each sentence. Check (✓) the right
answer.

	always	sometimes	never
1. I pay with cash.	_____	_____	_____
2. I pay with checks.	_____	_____	_____
3. I pay with credit cards.	_____	_____	_____
4. I have a lot of cash with me.	_____	_____	_____
5. I go shopping alone.	_____	_____	_____

B. Directions: This exercise is about you. Read each sentence. Circle *yes* or *no*.

1. I have some credit cards.	yes	no
2. I have a checking account.	yes	no
3. I have a lot of cash with me now.	yes	no
4. I think credit cards are safer than cash.	yes	no
5. I think credit cards are safer than checks.	yes	no
6. I think cash is easier to use than checks.	yes	no

Check-Up Unit Three: Lessons 8–11

Exercise 1: Understanding Sounds

Directions: Circle the word with the same sound as the letters underlined.

1. sleep   stop   slow
2. fireplace   police   plastic
3. blue   bill   block
4. phone   telephone   please

Exercise 2: Understanding Words

Directions: Match the pictures and the words. Write the right word next
to each picture.

total	signature	spoon	catalog

1. _____

2. _____

3. _____

4. _____

Exercise 3: Understanding Paragraphs

Directions: Read the narrative. Then answer the questions.

    Mary and Ellen have credit cards. Last month, Mary's
statement was for $53.20. Ellen's statement was for $321.00.
Mary could pay her bill, but Ellen couldn't pay hers.

1. How much did Mary spend last month?

_____

2. How much did Ellen spend?

_____

3. Who could not pay her bill?

_____

4. This paragraph shows that credit cards are dangerous.   Yes   No

Exercise 4: Careful Reading

Directions: Look at the pictures from the catalog and read the descriptions.
Then answer the questions.

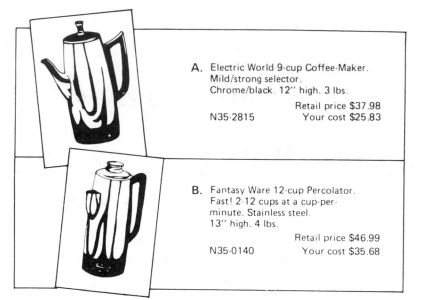

A. Electric World 9-cup Coffee-Maker.
Mild/strong selector.
Chrome/black. 12" high. 3 lbs.

N35-2815   Retail price $37.98
                       Your cost $25.83

B. Fantasy Ware 12-cup Percolator.
Fast! 2-12 cups at a cup-per-
minute. Stainless steel.
13" high. 4 lbs.

N35-0140   Retail price $46.99
                       Your cost $35.68

1. Who makes coffee-maker A? _____

2. How much does percolator B cost? _____

3. What is the catalog number of coffee-maker A? _____

4. What is the catalog number of percolator B? _____

5. Which model is cheaper?   A   B

6. Which model is made of stainless steel?   A   B

UNIT FOUR
Lifestyles

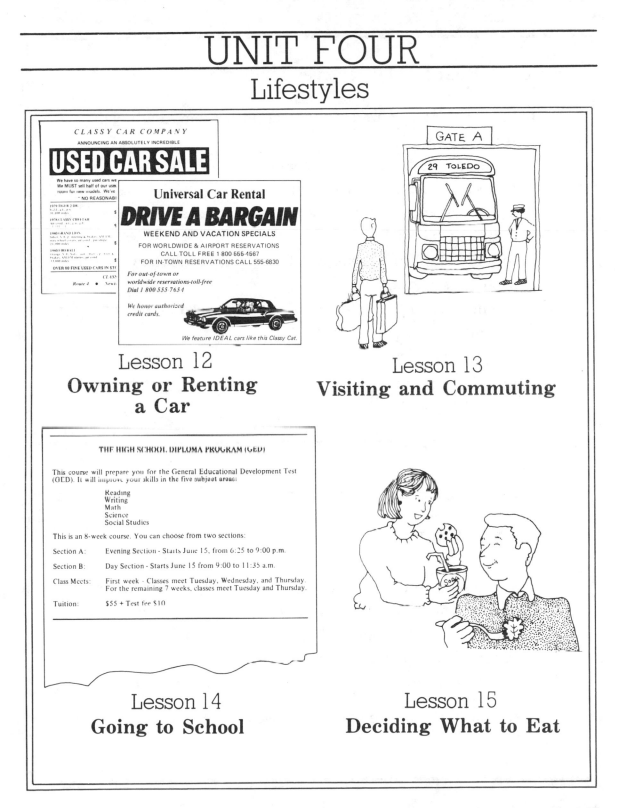

CLASSY CAR COMPANY

ANNOUNCING AN ABSOLUTELY INCREDIBLE

USED CAR SALE

We have so many used cars we
We MUST sell half of our used
room for new models. We've
"NO REASONABLE

1979 TIGER 2 DR.
6 cyl., a/c, p/s
35,000 miles

1978 CLASSY CHEETAH
air cond., a/c, p/s, p/b

1980 GRAND LION
4-door, V-8, p/steering & brakes, AM/FM
auto wheel covers, air cond., pin stripe
25,000 miles

1980 FIREBALL
Orange, V-8, 8-cyl., auto, 4 spd, a/c, 4-pwr
brakes, AM/FM stereo, air cond.
33,000 miles

OVER 80 FINE USED CARS IN STOCK

CLASS
Route 4 • Newt

Universal Car Rental

DRIVE A BARGAIN

WEEKEND AND VACATION SPECIALS

FOR WORLDWIDE & AIRPORT RESERVATIONS
CALL TOLL FREE 1 800 666-4567
FOR IN-TOWN RESERVATIONS CALL 555-6830

*For out-of-town or
worldwide reservations-toll-free
Dial 1 800 555 7654*

*We honor authorized
credit cards.*

We feature IDEAL cars like this Classy Cat.

Lesson 12
Owning or Renting a Car

GATE A

29 TOLEDO

Lesson 13
Visiting and Commuting

THE HIGH SCHOOL DIPLOMA PROGRAM (GED)

This course will prepare you for the General Educational Development Test
(GED). It will improve your skills in the five subject areas:

        Reading
        Writing
        Math
        Science
        Social Studies

This is an 8-week course. You can choose from two sections:

Section A: Evening Section - Starts June 15, from 6:25 to 9:00 p.m.

Section B: Day Section - Starts June 15 from 9:00 to 11:35 a.m.

Class Meets: First week - Classes meet Tuesday, Wednesday, and Thursday.
For the remaining 7 weeks, classes meet Tuesday and Thursday.

Tuition: $55 + Test fee $10

Lesson 14
Going to School

Lesson 15
Deciding What to Eat

Student Reading Objectives

1. to recognize and understand the inflectional endings:
   -er, -est, -s, -ed, -ing
2. to understand denotative meaning
3. to recall specific information
4. to understand the meaning of relevant vocabulary by using definition clues
5. to understand the meaning of relevant vocabulary by using synonyms and antonyms
6. to understand the meaning of relevant vocabulary by using summary clues
7. to make generalizations
8. to draw conclusions
9. to identify main ideas

ESL Information

The following intermediate-level grammatical structures are used and practiced for the first time in Unit Four.

1. infinitive structures
2. reported or indirect speech
3. the past perfect tense

A review of the present perfect tense also appears in this Unit.

Lesson 12 Owning or Renting a Car

Universal Car Rental

DRIVE A BARGAIN

WEEKEND AND VACATION SPECIALS

FOR WORLDWIDE & AIRPORT RESERVATIONS
CALL TOLL FREE 1 800-555-4567
FOR IN-TOWN RESERVATIONS CALL 555-6830

*For out-of-town or
worldwide reservations-toll-free
Dial 1-800-555-7654*

*We honor authorized
credit cards.*

We feature IDEAL cars like this Classy Cat.

CLASSY CAR COMPANY

ANNOUNCING AN ABSOLUTELY INCREDIBLE

USED CAR SALE

We have so many used cars we've literally run out of space.
We MUST sell half of our used car inventory THIS WEEK to make
room for new models. We've slashed prices but you can save even more.

"NO REASONABLE OFFER WILL BE REFUSED."

CLASSY CHEETAH	$4595	FIREBALL	
FALCON	$5395	CLASSY CHASSIS	$4995
	$6995	PANTHER	$5895
	$7295	CLASSY SAFARI WAGON	$6995
			$7395

USED CARS IN STOCK ALL AT SIMILAR LOW LOW SALE PRICES

CLASSY CAR COMPANY
Newtown   Exit 375 off Route 95

Joseph Mora is 38, married, and a police officer. Does he need to own a car?

Barbara Willis is 40, single, and a school teacher. Can she afford to own a car?

Barbara Willis doesn't need to own a car. She is 40 years old, single, and a school teacher. She doesn't earn much money, but she likes to travel a lot. She often rents a car. She prefers to rent a car on weekends because the prices are cheaper. She also usually rents a car for several weeks in the summer because she likes to take a vacation then.

Joseph Mora needs to own a car. He is 38 years old, married, and the father of two children. He is a police officer and his wife is a homemaker. Joseph's wife needs to use the car during the week. She has to take the children to school, go shopping, and do a lot of errands. On weekends, the family sometimes goes to a movie or a restaurant. In the summer, they often go to the beach on weekends.

1. Barbara Willis is married.   yes   no
2. Barbara likes to travel.   yes   no
3. Barbara often rents a car.   yes   no
4. Barbara prefers to rent a car on weekends.   yes   no
5. She usually rents a car during the winter.   yes   no
6. Does Barbara Willis need to own a car? Copy the sentence that answers this question.

1. Joseph Mora is a police officer.   yes   no
2. Joseph prefers to own a car.   yes   no
3. Joseph prefers to rent a car.   yes   no
4. He doesn't use the car on weekends.   yes   no
5. Mrs. Mora uses the car during the week.   yes   no
6. Does Joseph Mora need to own a car? Copy the sentence that answers this question.

Exercise 1: Careful Reading

Directions: Look at the two ads. Read about renting a car and buying a car. Then answer the questions.

Universal Car Rental

DRIVE A BARGAIN

WEEKEND AND VACATION SPECIALS

FOR WORLDWIDE & AIRPORT RESERVATIONS
CALL TOLL FREE 1-800-555-4567
FOR IN-TOWN RESERVATIONS CALL 555-6830

*For out-of-town or
worldwide reservations-toll-free
Dial 1-800-555-7654*

*We honor authorized
credit cards.*

We feature IDEAL cars like this Classy Cat.

CLASSY CAR COMPANY

ANNOUNCING AN ABSOLUTELY INCREDIBLE

USED CAR SALE

We have so many used cars we've literally run out of space. We MUST sell half of our used car inventory THIS WEEK to make room for new models. We've slashed prices but you can save even more. "NO REASONABLE OFFER WILL BE REFUSED."

1979 TIGER 2 DR.
6 cyl., a.t., p.s.
31,100 miles

1978 CLASSY CHEETAH   **$4595**
Air cond., a.t., p.s., p.b.
85,000 miles

1980 GRAND LION   **$5395**
Silver, V-8, p. steering & brakes, AM/FM,
wire wheel covers, air cond., pin stripe
21,900 miles

1980 FIREBALL
Orange, V-8, Auto. auto. trans., p. steer. &
brakes, AM/FM stereo, air cond.
33,000 miles   **$7295**

1979 FIREBALL
V6, 4 speed, AM/FM stereo w/8track
p.b., p.s., 28,000 miles

1979 CLASSY CHASSIS   **$4995**
Burgundy, auto. trans., 8 cyl., p. s., p.b.,
air cond., luggage rack   25,000 miles   **$5895**

1980 PANTHER
Silver, V-8, auto. trans., p. steering &
brakes, AM radio, rally wheels, air cond.
26,000 miles   **$6995**

1980 LION SAFARI WAGON
Brown, V-8, auto. trans., rallys, air con.,
AM/FM stereo, p. steering & brakes
24,000 miles   **$7395**

OVER 80 FINE USED CARS IN STOCK. ALL AT SIMILAR LOW, LOW SALE PRICES

CLASSY CAR COMPANY
Route 4   •   Newtown   •   555-2100
Exit 31S off Route 95

RENTING A CAR

1. What telephone numbers can you call for a car reservation in town?

   _____

   _____

2. Are there special prices for weekends and vacations?   yes   no

3. Can you use a credit card to pay?   yes   no

4. What telephone number can you call for a car reservation out-of-town?

   _____

5. Is this telephone call free?   yes   no

BUYING A CAR

6. Are these cars new or used?   _____

7. How much does the cheapest car cost?   _____

8. How much does the most expensive car cost?   _____

9. Where is the Classy Car Company?   _____

10. What is the Classy Car Company's telephone number?   _____

Exercise 2: Understanding Words

Directions: Find the opposite. Look at the example first. Then write the letter next to the right word.

1. new   _____C_____   a. out-of-town

2. weekend   _____   b. expensive

3. in town   _____   c. used

4. single   _____   d. summer

5. cheap   _____   e. married

6. winter   _____   f. weekday

Exercise 3: Understanding Word Endings

Directions: Add -er and -est to these words. Write the new words.

	er	est
1. cheap	_____	_____
2. new	_____	_____
3. high	_____	_____
4. small	_____	_____
5. strong	_____	_____
6. mild	_____	_____
7. short	_____	_____
8. few	_____	_____

Exercise 4: THINK

A. This exercise is about you. What do you need to **own** a car?

1. <u>You need money</u>. You can pay your own money or you can borrow some from a bank.

2. <u>You need a driver's license</u>. You can go to driver's school to get trained or someone you know who has a driver's license can teach you.

3. <u>You need car insurance</u>. If a thief steals your car, your insurance company will pay you money. If you have an accident, they will also pay you money. Car insurance is expensive.

4. <u>You need a license plate to put on your car</u>. First you must register your car at a Registry of Motor Vehicles office in your state. Then the registry will give you a license plate.

1. Do you have enough money to buy a car?   yes   no

2. Do you have a driver's license?   yes   no

3. Do you have enough money for car insurance?   yes   no

4. Do you have a license plate for your car?   yes   no

B. This exercise is about you. What do you need to **rent** a car?

1. <u>You need a driver's license.</u> You must be a licensed driver in order to drive a rental car.

2. <u>You need a reservation.</u> You must choose the date first. Then you must call the car rental agency and tell them the date.

3. <u>You need money.</u> You can pay cash. It is easier to pay with a credit card or by check.

1. Do you have a driver's license?   yes   no

2. Can you make a reservation?   yes   no

3. Do you have enough money?   yes   no

Lesson 13 Visiting and Commuting

This is a bus terminal. It's 7:00 P.M. on Friday. Wayne and Gina have just arrived. Why did they come? How did they read the bus timetable?

Hi! My name is Gina Russo and I live in Cleveland, Ohio. I have to go to Toledo every weekend for personal reasons. My mother is 60 years old and she lives in Toledo. She got sick a year ago, and so I go to visit her once a week. I've visited her every weekend for the last year. I took Bus 29 from Cleveland to Toledo today. Right now, it's Friday night and I've just arrived in Toledo. My father is waiting for me so I have to go. Good-bye.

Hello. My name is Wayne Tripp. I live in Toledo, Ohio, but I work in Cleveland. I have to commute to work in Cleveland every day. My family lives in Toledo, too. I couldn't find a job in Toledo, so I had to get a job in Cleveland. I've lived in Toledo for 30 years, and I've worked in Cleveland for two years. I come home to Toledo every weekend. Right now, I've just arrived in Toledo. I took Bus 29 from Cleveland this afternoon. My family is waiting for me so I have to go. Good-bye.

1. Gina Russo lives in Toledo.   yes   no
2. Gina's mother lives in Toledo.   yes   no
3. Gina has visited her mother every weekend
   for the last year.   yes   no
4. She arrived in Toledo yesterday.   yes   no
5. Her father is waiting for her.   yes   no
6. Why does Gina have to go to Toledo every weekend? Copy the sentence that answers this question.

1. Wayne Tripp works in Toledo and lives in
   Cleveland.   yes   no
2. He couldn't find a job in Toledo.   yes   no
3. Wayne's lived in Toledo for 20 years.   yes   no
4. He's worked in Cleveland for 6 months.   yes   no
5. His family is waiting for him now.   yes   no
6. Why does Wayne have to commute every day? Copy the sentence that answers this question.

Exercise 1: Careful Reading

Directions: Read the timetable. Answer the questions.

CLEVELAND - TOLEDO TIMETABLE

115	Read down 62	29		Bus number	115	Read up 62	29
daily▲ exc Sun	daily	Fri Sun only		Frequency	daily▲ exc Sun	daily	Fri Sun only
			Mi	Type of service			
7 15 a	8 30 a	5 00 p	0	Cleveland	6 00 p	11 00 a	9 25 p
↓	9 10 a		25	Rocky River		10 20 a	↑
d 8 10 a	9 35 a		52	Cedar Point	r5 05 p	9 55 a	
8 30 a	10 00 a	6 10 p	74	Elyria	4 45 p	9 30 a	8 02 p
8 35 a	10 15 a	6 25 p		Lakewood	4 40 p	9 15 a	7 52 p
	10 30 a		89	Bay Village		9 00 a	↑
9 00 a	10 42 a	↓	97	Fairview	4 15 p	8 48 a	
9 15 a	11 00 a	6 55 p	110	Toledo	4 00 p	8 30 a	7 30 p

Explanation of Symbols and Letters

a   a m (morning)
ar   arrive
d   Stops to discharge passengers only
dp   depart
n   noon
p   p m (afternoon)
r   Stops to receive passengers only

▲ Bus will not operate Dec. 25 Jan 1

1. Gina and Wayne took Bus 29 from Cleveland to Toledo. What time did it leave Cleveland? _____

2. What time did it arrive in Toledo? _____

3. Does Bus 115 go on Sundays?　　　　　　yes　　　　no

4. What time does Bus 62 leave Cleveland?　　_____

5. Does it leave in the afternoon?　　　　　yes　　　　no

6. When does Bus 29 leave Toledo for Cleveland? _____

7. When does it arrive in Cleveland?　　_____

8. When does it arrive in Elyria?　　_____

9. Does it leave in the morning?　　　　　yes　　　　no

10. Which bus leaves Toledo at 4:00 P.M.? _____

11. Which bus leaves Cleveland at 7:15 A.M.? _____

12. Gina and Wayne want to leave Toledo on Sunday evening. Which bus will they take? _____

Exercise 2: Understanding Words

Directions: Find the opposite. Write the letter next to the word.

1. slow	_____	a. out
2. in	_____	b. last
3. save	_____	c. spend
4. first	_____	d. fast
5. night	_____	e. man
6. woman	_____	f. day

Exercise 3: Understanding Word Endings

Directions: Complete the following.

1. Gina _____ her mother every weekend for the
   (visit)
   last year.

2. Wayne _____ in Toledo for 30 years.
   (live)

3. He's _____ in Cleveland for 2 years.
   (work)

4. They _____ just _____ in Toledo.
   (arrive)

5. You _____ just _____ this exercise.
   (finish)

Exercise 4: THINK

A. Directions: You want to travel between Chicago and Detroit. Use the timetable to answer the questions.

CHICAGO - DETROIT TIMETABLE						
	Read down			Read up		
	118	74	30	118	74	30
	daily	daily	daily exc - Sun	daily	daily	daily exc. Sun
Chicago	4:15 p	3:15 p	7:45 a	12:10 p	1:45 p	10:30 p
Niles	7:10 p			11:15 a		9:35 p
Kalamazoo	8:10 p	7:50 p	12:10	10:15 a		8:40 p
Ann Arbor	10:20 p		1:50 p		9:45 a	
Detroit	11:05 p	12:35 a	2:35 p	3:30 a	9:00 a	5:45 p

a a.m. (morning)   d Stops to discharge passengers only
p p.m. (afternoon)   r Stops to receive passengers only
n noon

1. When does Bus 118 leave Chicago?   _____

2. When does Bus 118 arrive in Detroit?   _____

3. Does Bus 118 stop in Niles?   yes   no

4. Does Bus 30 leave Chicago in the morning or afternoon?   _____

5. Does Bus 30 arrive in Detroit in the morning or afternoon?   _____

6. When does Bus 74 leave Detroit?   _____

7. When does Bus 74 arrive in Chicago?   _____

8. Which bus leaves Detroit at 3:30 A.M.?   _____

9. Which bus leaves Chicago at 7:45 A.M.?   _____

10. You want to arrive in Chicago Saturday night. Which bus will you take?   _____

11. Does Bus 118 go on Sundays?   yes   no

12. Does Bus 30 go on Sundays?   yes   no

B. Directions: These questions are about you. Circle the right answers.

1. Do you often travel by bus?   yes   no

2. Do you often travel by car?   yes   no

3. Do you often travel by train?   yes   no

4. Have you ever used a bus schedule?   yes   no

5. Have you ever used a train schedule?   yes   no

6. Do you own a car?   yes   no

7. Have you ever rented a car?   yes   no

8. Do you go to work by bus?   yes   no

9. Do you go to work by car?   yes   no

10. Do you visit your parents on weekends?   yes   no

11. Do you travel a lot on weekends?   yes   no

12. Do you travel a lot on weekdays?   yes   no

Lesson 14 **Going to School**

Dorothy Crane and Felipe Pérez are adult students. They are studying at a community college. What are they studying. Why are they studying?

Te-Wen Chang is a reporter. He writes for a newspaper. Last week he wrote an interesting article about adult students. He interviewed two people before he wrote the article. Here are his interviews with Dorothy Crane and Felipe Pérez.

Te-Wen Chang: What's your name?
Dorothy Crane: Dorothy Crane.
Te-Wen Chang: Why are you going to school?
Dorothy Crane: I want to be a better nurse.
Te-Wen Chang: Which class are you going to take?
Dorothy Crane: I'm going to take Spanish.
Te-Wen Chang: Why are you going to take Spanish?
Dorothy Crane: I'm a nurse. Many patients in the hospital speak Spanish. I want to speak Spanish, too. I want to be a bilingual nurse.

Te-Wen Chang: What's your name?
Felipe Pérez: Felipe Pérez
Te-Wen Chang: Why are you going to school?
Felipe Pérez: I want to get my high school diploma.
Te-Wen Chang: Which class are you going to take?
Felipe Pérez: I'm going to take math.
Te-Wen Chang: Why are you going to take math?
Felipe Pérez: I never graduated from high school. I need math to get my high school diploma.

1. Te-Wen Chang is a student.   yes   no

2. Te-Wen interviewed two students.   yes   no

3. Dorothy is going to take Spanish.   yes   no

4. Dorothy is a patient in a hospital. yes   no

5. Many hospital patients speak Spanish. yes   no

6. Dorothy wants to be bilingual.   yes   no

1. Felipe is going to take math.   yes   no

2. Felipe graduated from high school. yes   no

3. Felipe has his high school diploma. yes   no

4. Felipe wants his high school diploma. yes   no

Exercise 1: Careful Reading

Directions: Read Te-Wen's newspaper article. Answer the questions.

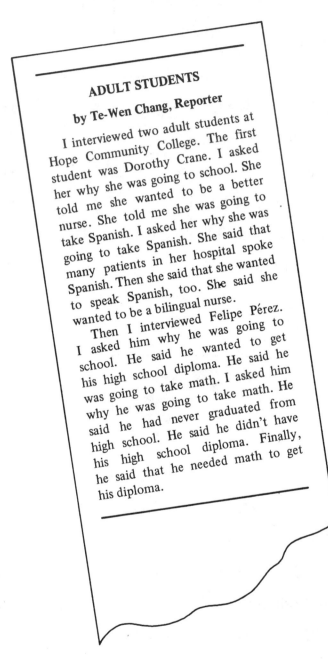

ADULT STUDENTS

by Te-Wen Chang, Reporter

I interviewed two adult students at Hope Community College. The first student was Dorothy Crane. I asked her why she was going to school. She told me she wanted to be a better nurse. She told me she was going to take Spanish. I asked her why she was going to take Spanish. She said that many patients in her hospital spoke Spanish. Then she said that she wanted to speak Spanish, too. She said she wanted to be a bilingual nurse.

Then I interviewed Felipe Pérez. I asked him why he was going to school. He said he wanted to get his high school diploma. He said he was going to take math. I asked him why he was going to take math. He said he had never graduated from high school. He said he didn't have his high school diploma. Finally, he said that he needed math to get his diploma.

1. What is Te-Wen Chang's occupation? _____

2. What is his article about? _____

3. Whom did he interview? _____

4. Can Dorothy Crane speak Spanish?   yes   no

5. Can Dorothy speak English?   yes   no

6. Is she bilingual now?   yes   no

7. Where did Te-Wen interview Dorothy and Felipe? _____

8. Has Felipe Pérez received his high school diploma?   yes   no

9. Does Felipe want his high school diploma?   yes   no

10. Did Felipe leave high school before he graduated?   yes   no

11. Why is Dorothy Crane going to school? Copy the sentence that answers this question.

_____

12. Why is Felipe Pérez going to school? Copy the sentence that answers this question.

_____

Exercise 2: Understanding Words

Directions: Find the word that means the same. Write the letter next to the word.

1. supermarket   _____   a. large

2. understand   _____   b. correct

3. phone   _____   c. store

4. price   _____   d. know

5. big   _____   e. cost

6. right   _____   f. telephone

Exercise 3: Understanding Word Endings

Directions: Add -ing to complete these sentences.

1. Susan walks to school every day. She is

_____ there now.
(walk)

2. James likes to look at TV. He is

_____ at it now.
(look)

3. Marvin interviews many people. He is

_____ now.
(interview)

4. Asha rents a car every weekend. She is

_____ one now.
(rent)

128

Exercise 4: THINK

Directions: Read the ad for the GED (General Educational Development) class. Answer the questions on the next page.

THE HIGH SCHOOL DIPLOMA PROGRAM (GED)

This course will prepare you for the General Educational Development Test (GED). It will improve your skills in the five subject areas:

Reading
Writing
Math
Science
Social Studies

This is an 8-week course. You can choose from two sections:

Section A: Evening Section - Starts June 15, from 6:25 to 9:00 p.m.

Section B: Day Section - Starts June 15 from 9:00 to 11:35 a.m.

Class Meets.   First week - Classes meet Tuesday, Wednesday, and Thursday. For the remaining 7 weeks, classes meet Tuesday and Thursday.

Tuition: $55 + Test fee $10

A. Questions about Donna

Donna saw the ad for a GED course and decided to take it. She went to the college, registered for Section A, and paid $65.00.

1. On what date is her first class? _____

2. What day of the week is June 15? _____

3. Will Donna go to this class on June 16?   yes   no

4. Why did Donna choose Section A?
   (Circle the right answer.)   a. She works during the day.

                                       b. She has to take care of her children during the day.

                                       c. We aren't sure.

B. Questions about you

   1. Do you have your high school diploma?   yes   no

   2. Have you ever taken a GED course?   yes   no

   3. Can you study during the day?   yes   no

   4. Can you study in the evening?   yes   no

   5. Can you afford a GED course?   yes   no

   6. Can you study twice a week?   yes   no

Lesson 15 Deciding What to Eat

Is Dan a vegetarian?
What is a vegetarian?

Has Kathy gained weight?
Why?

Dan Johnson became a vegetarian last year. He does not eat meat or poultry. Before he became a vegetarian he had been a typical American. He had eaten a lot of meat and poultry. Now he is different. He eats more fruit, like apples and oranges. He also eats a lot of vegetables, like lettuce, beans, and carrots. Sometimes he eats seafood, like fish. And he eats fewer carbohydrates, like bread and potatoes. A few weeks ago he saw that he had lost a lot of weight since he became a vegetarian. He also feels better now.

Kathy Robbins is a secretary. She changed jobs last year. Before she became a secretary she had been a mail carrier. She had delivered letters for the post office. When she was a mail carrier she walked 20 miles every day and ate a sandwich and some fruit for lunch. Now she sits all day. She has more time for lunch, so she eats more food. She also eats different kinds of food. Now she eats a lot of carbohydrates for lunch. She eats a sandwich, potato chips, cookies, and drinks a soda. She has gained ten pounds since last year.

1. Dan Johnson is a vegetarian.   yes   no
2. Dan eats meat.   yes   no
3. He eats a lot of fruits and vegetables.   yes   no
4. He eats more carbohydrates now.   yes   no
5. He lost a lot of weight.   yes   no

1. Kathy Robbins used to be a mail carrier.   yes   no
2. Kathy Robbins used to be a secretary.   yes   no
3. Now Kathy sits in a chair all day.   yes   no
4. She eats more now than she ate before.   yes   no
5. She eats fruit for lunch now.   yes   no

Exercise 1: Careful Reading

Directions: The chart below presents seven food groups. Read the chart.
Then answer the questions on the next page.

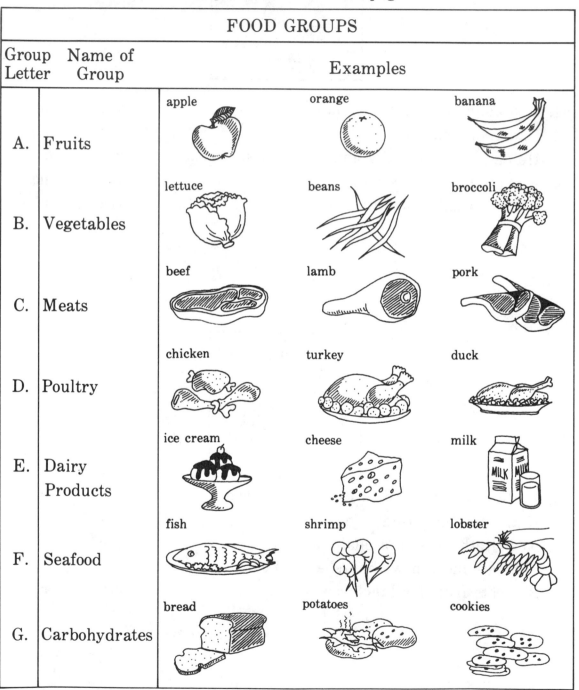

FOOD GROUPS		
Group Letter / **Name of Group**	**Examples**	
A. Fruits	apple / orange	banana
B. Vegetables	lettuce / beans	broccoli
C. Meats	beef / lamb	pork
D. Poultry	chicken / turkey	duck
E. Dairy Products	ice cream / cheese	milk
F. Seafood	fish / shrimp	lobster
G. Carbohydrates	bread / potatoes	cookies

1. An orange is a fruit.   yes   no

2. A shrimp is poultry.   yes   no

3. Lettuce is a vegetable.   yes   no

4. Ice cream is a carbohydrate.   yes   no

5. Broccoli is a fruit.   yes   no

6. Chicken is a meat.   yes   no

7. Potatoes are a carbohydrate.   yes   no

8. Lamb is a meat.   yes   no

9. Cheese is seafood.   yes   no

10. Beef is poultry.   yes   no

11. Write two examples of poultry.   _____

                                             _____

12. Write three examples of vegetables.   _____

                                             _____

                                             _____

Exercise 2: Understanding Words

Directions: Find the opposite. Write the letter next to the right word.

1. big	_____	a.	little
2. yes	_____	b.	wrong
3. right	_____	c.	no
4. large	_____	d.	arrive
5. old	_____	e.	small
6. leave	_____	f.	young

Exercise 3: Understanding Word Endings

Directions: Add -s to each word. Look at the example first.

1. one hamburger	two	*hamburgers*
2. one apple	one dozen	_____
3. one salad	three	_____
4. one day	seven	_____
5. one pound	ten	_____
6. one chair	four	_____
7. one turkey	five	_____

Exercise 4: THINK

A.   Choices about food are very important. These choices are important for your health, your appearance, and your family's health and appearance. Every day you make three kinds of choices about food. First, you decide how many meals and snacks you are going to eat. Will you eat breakfast, lunch, and dinner? Will you eat lunch, dinner, and a snack in the evening? Second, you decide how much you are going to eat. Will your meals be large or small? Third, you decide the kind of food you are going to eat.

   Some doctors divide food into seven groups. They say that every person should eat something from each group every day. They say you need these foods for good health.

SEVEN FOOD GROUPS

1. dairy products
2. meat, fish, poultry, eggs, and dried beans
3. green and yellow vegetables
4. citrus fruits (oranges, lemons, grapefruit), tomatoes
5. other fruits, potatoes, and other vegetables not in Group 3
6. bread, cereals, and pasta (spaghetti)
7. butter, margarine, or oil

Directions: What choices are very important?

1. Copy the sentence that answers this question.

_____

2. What are three kinds of decisions you make about food every day?

_____

_____

_____

3. Food is important for your health.   yes   no

4. Some doctors divide food into six groups.   yes   no

B. Directions: Answer these questions about your food choices.

1. How many meals do you eat every day? _____

2. How many snacks do you eat every day? _____

3. Are your meals small, average, or large? _____

4. Do you eat Group 1 foods every day?   yes   no

5. Do you eat Group 2 foods every day?   yes   no

6. Do you eat Group 3 foods every day?   yes   no

7. Do you eat Group 4 foods every day?   yes   no

8. Do you eat Group 5 foods every day?   yes   no

9. Do you eat Group 6 foods every day?   yes   no

10. Do you eat Group 7 foods every day?   yes   no

11. Do you eat something from each group every day?   yes   no

12. What is your favorite food? _____

13. Which group is it in? _____

14. Do you eat a lot of meat?   yes   no

15. Are you a vegetarian?   yes   no

Check-Up Unit Four: Lessons 12-15

Exercise 1: Understanding Words

A. Directions: Find the word that means the opposite. Write the letter next to the word.

1. in _____   a. first

2. cheap _____   b. new

3. last _____   c. expensive

4. used _____   d. man

5. woman _____   e. out

B. Directions: Find the word that means the same. Write the letter next to the word.

1. small _____   a. little

2. right _____   b. big

3. large _____   e. go

4. leave _____   d. correct

5. understand _____   e. know

Exercise 2: Careful Reading

A. Directions: Read the narrative. Then answer the questions.

My name is Lucy Smith and I live in Cleveland. I have to go to Toledo every weekend. My father is 65 years old and he lives in Toledo. He got sick two years ago. I go to visit him every weekend. I take Bus 29 from Cleveland to Toledo every Friday.

1. Lucy Smith lives in Toledo.   yes   no

2. Lucy's father lives in Toledo.   yes   no

3. Lucy visits her father every weekend.   yes   no

4. Her mother is waiting for her.   yes   no

5. Why does Lucy have to go to Toledo every weekend? Copy the sentences that answer this question.

_____

_____

B. Directions: Read the narrative. Then answer the questions.

    My name is David Jones. I live in Boston but I work in Providence. I have to commute to work every day. My family lives in Boston, too. I couldn't find a job in Boston, so I had to get a job in Providence. I've lived in Boston for 30 years and I've worked in Providence for two years. I come home to Boston every night.

1. David Jones works in Boston and lives in Providence.   yes   no

2. He couldn't find a job in Providence.   yes   no

3. He's lived in Boston for 20 years.   yes   no

4. He's worked in Providence for six months.   yes   no

5. His family lives in Boston.   yes   no

6. Why does David have to commute every day? Copy the sentence that answers this question.

_____

_____

140

APPENDIX: VOCABULARY FROM *IMPACT!* BOOK 1

A
a
able
above
accept
account
across
address
after
afternoon
age
ahead
all
am
an
and
another
answer
anything
apartment
apples
apply
appointment
are
aren't
ask
at
attend

B
bank
basement
bathroom
bedroom
bedtime
begin
behind
below
big
bills
birth
blocks
blouse
born
boss
bottles
bought
bread

breakfast
brother
brother-in-law
building
bus
busy
but
buying

C
call
came
can
can't
car
cart
cash
cashier
cat
cents
change
cheap
check
checkout
chicken
children
classes
cleaning
clerks
clothes
clothing
coat
coffee
coming
cook
cooking
corn
corner
costs
counter

D
date
daughter
day
degrees
desk
did

different
dinner
directions
divorced
do
doctor
does
doesn't
dollar
don't
dress
drive
driver

E
eating
eggs
eight
electric
employers
empty
ends
enough
every
everything
exact
excuse
expensive

F
family
fare
father
father-in-law
feel
few
fifty
fill
fine
fire
firemen
first
fish
floor
food
for
form
former

four
fourth
french fries
friend
from
front
full-time

G
gas
get
girls
give
giving
going
good
grandmother

H
hamburger
has
have
he
head
health
heat
hello
help
her
here
he's
high
him
his
hospital
hot
hour
house
how
hungry
hurts
husband

I
I
I'm
in
include

information
inside
insurance
is
isn't
it
it's

J
jacket
janitor
job

K
kitchen
know

L
landlord
large
last
learn
left
liquor
living
long
look
lose
lost
lot
luck
lunch

M
mail
make
man
manager
many
married
me
meat
medicine
medium
meet
men
menu
middle
milk
minutes
money

month
morning
mother
mother-in-law
much
my

N
name
need
neighbor
new
next
night
nineteen
no
not
now
number
nurse

O
occupation
o'clock
of
office
old
on
one
only
or
order
our
out
owe

P
paid
parents
parking
pay
people
pharmacist
pharmacy
playing
please
police
police officer
post office
pound
prescriptions

price

Q
questions

R
reading
refill
refuse
register
registration
renting
restaurant
rice
right
room

S
sale
sandwich
save
savings
school
second
secretary
security
see
semester
she
she's
shirt
shoe
shopping
sick
side
sign
single
sister
sitting
size
skirt
slacks
sleep
sleepy
slowly
small
social
soda
son
son-in-law
soup

speak
spend
starts
station
stomach
stop
store
straight
street
student
studying
suit
supermarket
sweater

T
taxes
tables
tablets
take
talking
tea
telephone
temperature
thank
that's
the
their
them
then
there
these
they
they're
think
third
this
three
times
to
today
tomorrow
too
traffic light
two
typing

U
understand
underwear
unemployment

use

V
very

W
wait
waiter
waitress
walk
want
was
watching
water
we
wear
week
well
went
were
what
when
where
who
whose
why
wife
will
with
woman
women
working
writing
wrote

X
—

Y
year
yes
you
young
your

Z
—

TIME ELEMENTS AND NUMBERS

1 one
2 two
3 three
4 four
5 five
6 six
7 seven
8 eight
9 nine
0 zero (optional)
a.m.
p.m.
noon
midnight
clock
o'clock

DAYS OF THE WEEK
Sunday
Monday
Tuesday
Wednesday
Thursday
Friday
Saturday

MONTHS OF THE YEAR
January
February
March
April
May
June
July
August
September
October
November
December

USA MONEY SYMBOLS AND TERMS
$ dollar(s)
¢ cent(s)
. (decimal point)
penny/.01/one cent/1¢
nickel/.05/five cents/5¢
dime/.10/ten cents/10¢
quarter/.25/twenty-five cents 25¢
half-dollar/.50/fifty cents/50¢

SPECIAL VOCABULARY
Abbreviations
Dr.
Mr.
Mrs.
No. (number)
R. Ph. (registered pharmacist)

Medicine Label and Prescription Terms
cause
daily
dosage
drowsiness
medications
operating
Ornade
Penicillin
reach
WARNING!

School Registration Form Terms and Phrases
amount
authorization
ball-point pen
bear down
continuing
division
education
financial aid
late fee
please print clearly
previously attended
receipt
sex: M–Male F–Female
status
total
tuition
type

Supermarket Terms
entrance
exit
special

Unemployment Form
Terminology
account number
Answer all questions
    carefully.
Claims are investigated.
Do not write in
    this block.
False statements can bring
    a fine or jail or both.
penalties of perjury
Present to claims taker.
signature
Weekly Benefit Statement